# crochet a Zoo

## fun toys for baby and you

Megan Kreiner

Martingale®

Create with Confidence

D122725

# Dedication

For my grandmother Amelia and my mother, Nancy.
It has been a privilege to carry on our family tradition.

Crochet a Zoo: Fun Toys for Baby and You
© 2013 by Megan Kreiner

Martingale®
19021 120th Ave. NE, Suite 102
Bothell, WA 98011 USA
ShopMartingale.com

Printed in China

18 17 16 15 14 13        8 7 6 5 4 3 2 1

Library of Congress Cataloging-in-Publication Data is available upon request.

ISBN: 978-1-60468-273-1

## Mission Statement

Dedicated to providing quality products and service to inspire creativity.

## Credits

PRESIDENT & CEO: Tom Wierzbicki

EDITOR IN CHIEF: Mary V. Green

DESIGN DIRECTOR: Paula Schlosser

MANAGING EDITOR: Karen Costello Soltys

ACQUISITIONS EDITOR: Karen M. Burns

TECHNICAL EDITOR: Ursula Reikes

COPY EDITOR: Marcy Heffernan

PRODUCTION MANAGER: Regina Girard

COVER & TEXT DESIGNER: Connor Chin

ILLUSTRATORS: Sue Mattero, Cheryl Falls, Megan Kreiner, and Adrienne Smitke

PHOTOGRAPHER: Brent Kane

# Contents

# Introduction

There's something very special about handmade toys. They become something to treasure for years to come and you can feel all warm and fuzzy about the care you've taken in selecting the projects and materials, and in adding your own special touches.

When I was expecting my son, I wanted to create toys that were not only safe, but also unique, inspiring, and fun. So, I set to work on a little crocheted lion. That lion was quickly followed by a giraffe and an elephant, and then a zebra and a hippopotamus. Soon, I had an entire zoo on my hands!

I'm thrilled to be able to share these patterns with you, and I hope that you'll enjoy creating these little animals and their keepers for the special people in your life.

# Crochet Basics

If you're just getting started with your first crochet project, this section is for you. When it comes to materials for your projects, always keep in mind quality over quantity. You don't need much yarn to make these toys, so it's worth using the best-quality materials for your special projects.

### YARN AND GAUGE

Choosing a yarn for your project is part of the fun of personalizing your creation! It's always a good idea to keep the age of your recipient in mind when choosing what kind of yarn to use. For very young children who like to put everything in their mouths, it might be prudent to go with organic or natural fibers, such as cotton or wool (but always be sure to check for allergies first).

Blended yarns are wonderful, as they often combine the best qualities of their respective fibers. Acrylic yarns can also make excellent toys as they are fairly easy to clean and care for and are generally less expensive than natural-fiber yarns.

Depending on what size you want your toy to be, you can choose a lighter or heavier yarn weight to achieve the desired results. For example, if you wish to make a family of elephants, you could use sport- or DK-weight yarn and a size D-3 (3.25 mm)

or E-4 (3.5 mm) hook to make calf versions of the original, or go jumbo by using bulky-weight yarn and a size I-9 (5.5 mm) hook. Refer to the standard yarn weights chart on page 78 for more information on yarn weights.

Most of the patterns in this book call for worsted-weight yarn, but you may find that the gauge of worsted-weight yarns can vary quite a bit in thickness from one brand to the next. Feel free to adjust your hook size accordingly so that your stitches stay close together. It's always better to err on the side of caution by going with a smaller hook, since you want your stitches to be fairly tight to prevent the stuffing from showing through.

As a general rule of thumb, 125 yards of worsted-weight yarn should be more than enough to make one toy. For pieces that require contrasting colors for paws, teeth, muzzles, and toenails, an additional 15 to 20 yards of those colors should do the trick.

Elephant stitched in bulky-, worsted-, and DK-weight yarn (from left to right)

## STUFFING

As with yarns, there are a variety of toy stuffings to choose from. Most craft and fabric stores carry polyester fiberfill, although more locations now carry natural fiber and organic options as well. The Internet can also be a great resource for specialty toy stuffing, such as organic wool and organic cotton.

For the toys in this book, I've used the following stuffing and batting:

- Hobbs Bonded Fibers polydown fiberfill toy stuffing (super soft and very nice to work with)
- NearSea Naturals organic wool stuffing
- NearSea Naturals organic cotton stuffing

Fiberfill, cotton, and wool toy stuffings (from left to right)

Sadly, black stuffing for dark-colored toys seems to be a rather scarce commodity, and, unless your stitches are super tight, white stuffing tends to show through, which can be an undesirable look. For black and brown toys, we have other options.

- An old black T-shirt cut up into little pieces can make effective stuffing. And it's thrifty!
- If you don't require too much black stuffing, you could use black wool roving. It may be a bit pricey, but it can be a good way to go if you wish to use only natural or organic materials in your project.
- Turn black cotton batting, like Hobbs Bonded Fibers Heirloom 80/20 Black Cotton Blend Quilt Batting, into stuffing. Simply cut off a chunk of batting and brush the heck out of it with a pet-grooming slicker brush (page 8). The result is clumps of black fluffiness that can then be used in your toy. It's a bit of work, but the result is pretty effective. Just make sure you place a scrap cloth under your batting before you start brushing so you don't scratch your work surface. If you don't have a brush handy, you can also use scissors to cut the batting into little ½" to 1" pieces.

- Around Halloween you may come across a product called "Halloween Hay" from Polyester Fibers, LLC, which is essentially black polyester fiberfill. If you find it, stock up!

### Noisemakers

To add a little more zing to your toy, you can also purchase toy-safe noisemakers like bells, squeakers, or rattles to insert into the body of your animal.

Noisemakers from American Felt and Craft

## CROCHET HOOKS

Crochet hooks vary in size, color, and material. I prefer metal hooks, because they're strong and don't bend while stitching. If you can, try to hold the hooks in your hand before you make your purchase to ensure a comfortable fit.

For the most accurate sizing, go by the millimeter sizing on the hook since different manufacturers use a range of markings and systems like numbers or letters. (See "Crochet Hook Sizes" on page 78 for hook sizes.) I used a G-6 (4 mm) hook for the majority of the projects. Because you're making stuffed animals and not garments, your stitch gauge and overall sizing is not crucial. Just be sure you're crocheting a firm fabric that won't allow stuffing to show through.

If you find your hand feels sore after crocheting for an extended period of time, it may be worth checking out the various lines of ergonomic hooks.

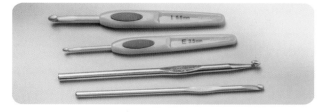

Assortment of crochet hooks. Notice that the ergonomic ones have a wider grip than traditional crochet hooks.

## STITCH COUNTERS AND SLIP RINGS

Because most of these patterns are worked in a continuous spiral, a stitch or row counter combined with the use of slip rings or safety pins marking the beginning of each round can help you keep track of which round you are currently working on.

Keep track of your progress easily with the help of stitch markers and a row/stitch counter.

## STICKY NOTES AND PENCILS

I always keep a small stack of sticky notes in my notions bag along with an automatic pencil. That way, when I need to stop midway through a project, I can stick a note right on the page in my pattern book and jot down exactly where I left off in the pattern. I'll sometimes just draw an arrow on the sticky note and line up the arrow with my current row so I can easily find my place when I come back to my project.

## PLASTIC EYES WITH SAFETY BACKINGS

Plastic eyes with safety backings are available at craft stores and on the Internet. My favorite online resource is etsy shop 6060, where you can pick up a variety of hard-to-find sizes and colors. The plastic backings, once applied, are designed not to accidentally come off again (see page 17). However, for children under three, I strongly recommend using felt circles or French knots for eyes (see page 16), as the plastic eyes can become a choking hazard if removed.

A variety of plastic safety eyes from etsy shop 6060

## FELT AND THREAD

As with yarns and toy stuffing, you have options when choosing felt and thread for your projects. Craft felt comes in a variety of colors and fiber contents, such as polyester, acrylic, wool, and bamboo. You can choose thread that matches your felt, or you can go for a fun patchwork look and use a contrasting color.

When tracing shapes onto felt, I find that a ballpoint pen or blunted No. 2 pencil works fairly well on light-colored felts, while a white gel pen works best on darker colors.

A selection of wool and bamboo felt from American Felt and Craft. Organic threads from NearSea Naturals, and traditional cotton threads from Gütermann.

## CUTTING TOOLS

Consider investing in a high-quality pair of scissors for cutting out felt shapes, and a smaller pair of embroidery scissors for trimming threads and loose ends. A sharp pair of scissors can make a big difference when cutting out felt patches and trimming hair and manes. Regardless of what brand you choose, use these scissors only on your crochet projects to keep the blade nice and sharp.

In addition, a craft utility knife and a small self-healing cutting mat (available at your local craft or quilting shop) can also make cutting out felt shapes cleaner and easier.

## STEEL NEEDLES

A few steel tapestry needles will make assembling your animals a snap. Skip the plastic tapestry needles, since they can sometimes bend when going through thick materials like felt or a tightly stuffed toy. Sew pattern pieces together and make French-knot eyes using a large tapestry needle with worsted-weight yarn, and a smaller tapestry needle with DK- or sport-weight yarn. For easier threading, look for needles with big eyes.

A size 20 or 22 embroidery or chenille needle is good for sewing on eyes and embroidering other details.

## SLICKER BRUSH

You can find slicker brushes in various pet stores, and it can be a very handy tool if you find yourself making lots of furry crocheted toys. I sometimes make finished toys fuzzier by dragging a small 3" brush along the surface to draw up the fibers. The brush can also be a helpful tool to loosen strands of novelty fun-fur yarn after it's been crocheted on for manes and hair. Most recently, I've been using my slicker brush to break up black quilt batting to use as stuffing for my black and brown toys (see "Stuffing" on page 6).

Soft wire slicker brush and brushed Hobbs black cotton-blend quilt batting

# Crochet Stitches

This section will provide an overview of all the stitches used for the patterns in this book. Since most of the patterns use only a few basic stitches, they make great projects for beginners.

## SLIPKNOT

❶ Make a loop with your yarn leaving a 6" tail.

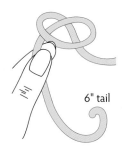

6" tail

❷ Insert the hook into the loop and gently pull up and tighten the yarn around the hook. The tail will be woven into your finished piece.

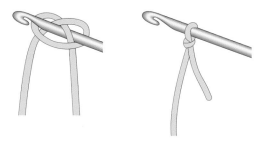

## YARN OVER (YO)

Wrap the yarn over your hook from back to front.

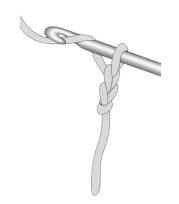

## FOUNDATION CHAIN (ch)

Start by making a slipknot and placing it on your hook. You'll have one loop on your hook.

❶ Yarn over the hook with the working yarn.

❷ Catch the yarn with your hook and draw it through the loop on your hook. You will now have a new loop on your hook with the slipknot below it. This is your first or "foundation" chain.

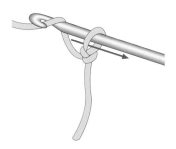

❸ Repeat steps 1 and 2 to make as many chains as indicated in the pattern. When checking your count, keep in mind that you should skip the loop currently on the hook and only count the chains below it.

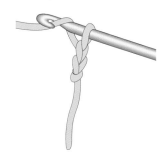

## SLIP STITCH (sl st)

Slip stitches can be used to move yarn across multiple stitches without adding additional height to the row. Start by inserting your hook into the next chain or stitch, yarn over the hook, and pull through both loops on the hook in one motion. You'll have one remaining loop on your hook.

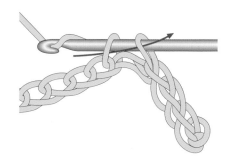

## SINGLE CROCHET (sc)

**❶** Insert your hook into the next chain or stitch in the pattern, yarn over the hook, and pull through the chain or stitch. You'll have two loops on your hook.

**❷** Yarn over the hook and pull through both loops on your hook to complete the stitch. You'll have one loop on your hook.

## HALF DOUBLE CROCHET (hdc)

**❶** Yarn over the hook and insert the hook into the next chain or stitch in the pattern. Yarn over the hook again and pull through the chain or stitch. You'll have three loops on your hook.

**❷** Yarn over the hook and pull through all three loops on the hook to complete the stitch. You'll have one loop on your hook.

## DOUBLE CROCHET (dc)

**❶** Yarn over the hook and insert the hook into the next chain or stitch in the pattern.

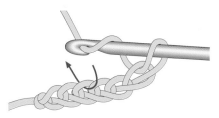

**❷** Yarn over the hook again and pull through the chain or stitch. You'll have three loops on your hook.

**❸** Yarn over the hook and pull through two loops on the hook. You'll have two loops remaining on the hook.

**❹** Yarn over the hook and pull through the last two loops on the hook to complete the stitch. You'll have one loop on your hook.

**4** Yarn over the hook and pull through the last two loops on the hook to complete the stitch. You'll have one loop on your hook.

## SINGLE-CROCHET INCREASES

You'll see most of the patterns in this book indicate "sc 2 in next sc" when an increase is needed. To work an increase, simply work the number of stitches specified into the same stitch.

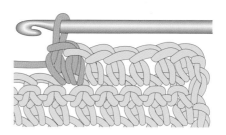

## SINGLE-CROCHET DECREASES (sc2tog)

All the patterns in this book use single-crochet decreases.

**1** Insert your hook into the next stitch, yarn over the hook, and pull through the stitch, leaving a loop on your hook. You'll have two loops on your hook.

**2** Repeat step 1 in the next stitch. You'll have three loops on your hook.

**3** Yarn over the hook and pull through all three loops. You'll have one loop on your hook.

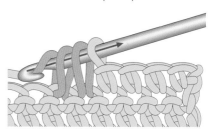

## TRIPLE CROCHET (tr)

**1** Yarn over the hook twice and insert the hook into the next chain or stitch in the pattern. Yarn over the hook and pull through the chain or stitch. You'll have four loops on your hook.

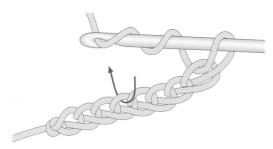

**2** Yarn over the hook and pull through two loops on the hook. You'll have three loops on your hook.

**3** Yarn over the hook and pull through two loops on the hook. You'll have two loops on your hook.

## ADJUSTABLE RING

The adjustable ring is a great technique that can take care of the unsightly hole in the middle of your starting round.

**❶** Form a ring with your yarn, leaving a 6" tail. Insert the hook into the loop as shown, as if you were making a slipknot.

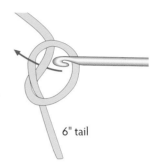

6" tail

**❷** Yarn over the hook and pull through the loop to make a slip stitch.

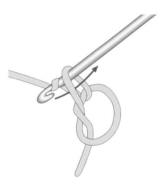

**❸** Chain one and then single crochet the number of stitches indicated in the pattern, taking care to enclose both strands of yarn that make up the adjustable ring. To close the center of the ring, pull tightly on the 6" yarn tail. Your adjustable ring is now complete.

To start your next round, work your next stitch in the first single crochet of the adjustable ring. If you need to make a semicircle shape (like for an ear), you'll be instructed to chain one and turn the work so that the wrong side of the work is facing you. You can then crochet into the single crochet stitches of the adjustable ring as indicated in the pattern.

## WORKING IN A SPIRAL ROUND

The patterns in this book are worked in a spiral round in which there is no slip stitch or chains between rounds. You just keep right on crocheting from one round to the next. To help keep track of the round that you are currently on, it can be helpful to make use of stitch markers and row counters.

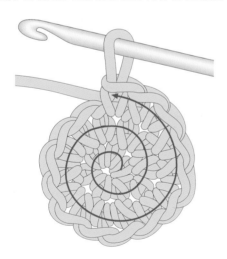

To keep track of the round you are currently on, you can use stitch markers and row counters. Place a stitch marker in the last stitch of the round you just worked. You'll know you've come to the end of a round when you get to the stitch with the marker. After removing the marker, work the last stitch in the round, replace the marker in the new last stitch, and proceed to the first stitch of the next round.

## WORKING AROUND A CHAIN

A few patterns begin by working around a chain of stitches. After creating your chain, you'll first work in the back ridge loops of the chain and then in the front loops of the chain. Let's walk through the steps in making an ear shape.

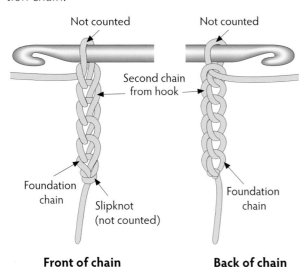

**❶** Make a chain as per the pattern instructions. The first chain st after the slipknot will be your "foundation chain."

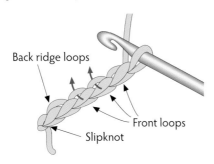

**Front of chain**      **Back of chain**

**❷** For round 1, starting in the second chain from the hook, work your first stitch in the back ridge loop of the chain. Continue working the pattern into the back ridge loops of the chain until you've reached the back ridge loop of the first foundation chain.

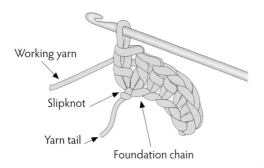

**❸** When you're ready to work the other side of the chain, rotate your work so the front loops are facing up. Starting in the next chain from the foundation chain, insert your hook under the two front loops of the chain st to work your stitch.

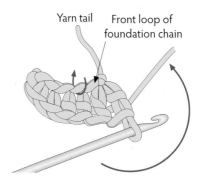

Rotate and work in front loops of chain.

**❹** Continue in the pattern until you reach the first stitch of round 1. You can now tie off your yarn to complete the ear shape. For patterns that instruct you to continue on to round 2, work your next stitch into the first stitch of round 1.

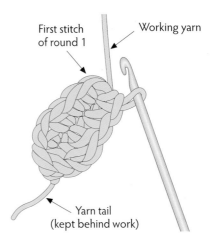

## CHECKING YOUR STITCH COUNT

Occasionally, you may want to count the stitches on your current round to make sure you have the correct number as you're going along. The basic rule of thumb to remember is that the loop on the hook does not count as a stitch.

## RIGHT SIDE (RS) VERSUS WRONG SIDE (WS)

It's important to keep track of which side of your pattern is the right side, as it will affect which part of the stitch you'll perceive as the back loop versus the front loop. Since most of the pattern pieces begin with an adjustable ring, the 6" tail left over from forming the ring will usually lie on the wrong side of the piece. The same can be said for patterns started by working around a chain, if you take care to keep the 6" yarn tail behind your work as you crochet.

## BACK LOOPS (BL) AND FRONT LOOPS (FL)

Unless otherwise indicated, you'll be working in both loops of a stitch except when the pattern instructs that a stitch should be worked in the back loop or front loop. When viewing your piece from the right side, the back loop will be the loop farthest away while the front loop is the loop closest to you.

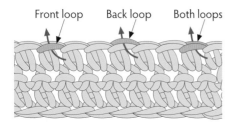

Front loop  Back loop  Both loops

## FASTENING OFF

After you've completed your last stitch, cut the yarn, leaving at least a 6"-long tail. To fasten the yarn off, draw this tail through the last loop on your hook and pull firmly to secure it. In many cases, you can use the long tail to sew other pieces to the body or to sew up a seam.

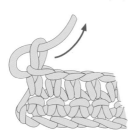

## CHANGING COLORS

Changing colors requires a little reading ahead when working your patterns, since a new color is actually introduced while you are completing the last stitch of the old color.

Work the stitch prior to the color change up to the last step in which you would normally pull the yarn through the loop(s) on your hook to complete the stitch. Proceed to swap out your old color for a new color and draw the new color through your loop(s) to complete the stitch. The result will be a loop of the new color on your hook. You can then continue on to the next stitch in the new color.

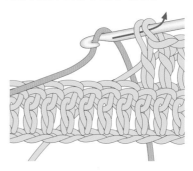

When introducing a second color, leave at least a 6" yarn tail that you can tie to the first yarn color on the wrong side of the work to avoid any gaps caused by loose strands at the site of the color change.

## CROCHETING ON THE SURFACE

Crocheting on the surface of your piece is a great way to add little details like hair, sleeve cuffs, and shirt collars to your creations. Patterns that call for this technique will use it in a very free-form kind of way so that the stitches are simply placed wherever you think they should go.

❶ On the right side of your work, insert your hook through the surface stitches of your piece, yarn over the hook and draw a loop back out through the surface stitches. You'll have one loop on your hook.

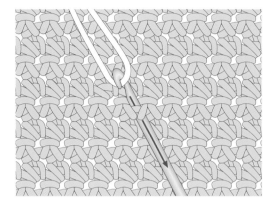

❷ Insert your hook into a space very close to your starting point and draw out another loop of yarn through the surface of your piece. You'll have two loops on your hook. Yarn over the hook in preparation for making the single crochet in the next step.

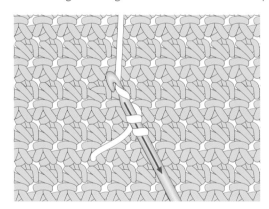

❸ Pull the yarn through the two loops. You've just made a single crochet on the surface of your piece. Yarn over the hook for the next stitch.

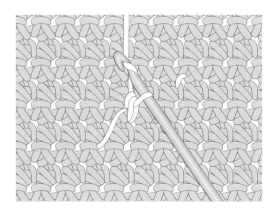

❹ Repeat steps 2 and 3 to create a free-form line of single crochet along the surface of your piece. Depending on the pattern instructions, you may continue to work additional rows into these stitches. Fasten off and weave in ends when finished.

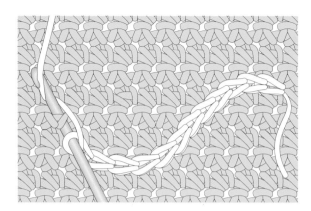

# Embroidery Stitches

Simple embroidery stitches are useful for adding noses,
eyes, eyebrows, and felt pieces.

### RUNNING STITCH

Use a running stitch to sew on eye circles and belly
patches. Simply pass the needle and thread in and
out of the fabric in a dashed-line pattern.

### SATIN STITCH

The satin stitch is used to create the nose shapes
on some animals, as well as toenails, and cheeks on
others. To make a basic nose, start by drawing the
yarn through the surface of your work from point
A to B and loop back around to reinsert the needle
next to point A (the beginning of the last stitch).
Work your satin stitches from point A to B, repeat
for shorter stitches from C to D, and then from E to
F taking care to keep the yarn and stitches very close
together. To make toenails, make stitches from E to
F five times.

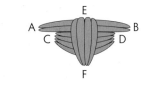

Nose

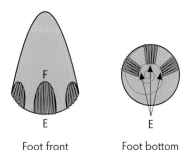

Foot front          Foot bottom

### LAZY DAISY STITCH

To create a pleasing curved eyebrow, I like to use a
variation of the lazy daisy stitch. Draw the yarn and
needle through the surface of your work at point A
where you would like the arch or eyebrow to begin.
Reinsert the needle where you would like the arch
to end at point B and very loosely draw the needle
through the work. Make small adjustments to the
loose yarn on the surface to form a nice arch. To
secure the arched shape, draw the needle through
at the top of the arch at point C and back down
through the surface at point D, making a small stitch
to hold the arch in place.

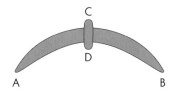

### FRENCH KNOT

French-knot eyes can be used in place of plastic
safety eyes. With the yarn and needle on the right
side of the work, hold the yarn close to the surface of
the work where the yarn has most recently emerged
and wind the yarn around the needle four or five
times (depending on how big an eye you would like
to make). While still applying tension to the yarn,
insert the needle close to where the yarn has most
recently emerged. Pull the needle through the work,
leaving a small knot on the surface.

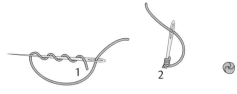

French knot (4 wraps)

# Finishing Touches

For the best results when putting your toy together, follow these final tips.

### WHIPSTITCH

The whipstitch is useful for closing seams in a nice neat line and for sewing your animal together. To close the openings on arms and legs, pinch the open edges together with your fingers. Using your tapestry needle and leftover yarn tail, draw your needle and yarn through your piece making sure to catch both edges. Pull the yarn up and over the edge of the work before pulling the needle through both edges again, in a spiral-like motion. Continue until the seam is closed or the piece is attached.

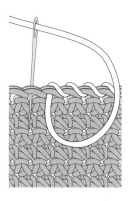

### CLOSING HOLES

For closing round holes like the ones on heads and body shapes, start by threading the remaining yarn tail onto a tapestry needle. Following the edge of the opening, insert the needle through each space and over the next single crochet, effectively winding the tail around the stitches. When you've gone all the way around the opening, pull the tail firmly to close the hole (just like you were cinching a drawstring bag closed).

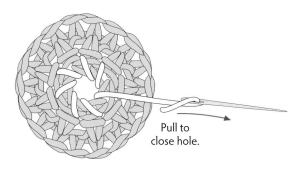

Pull to close hole.

### ATTACHING BODY PARTS

After you've closed up your seams, you can begin to assemble your toy! For legs and arms, lay the closed seams flat against the body and whipstitch them in place with the leftover yarn tail. If you find it tricky to keep the leg placement even, use a couple of large pins (called marking pins) to pin your legs into position to make sure your placement will work before you start sewing everything in place.

To attach pieces that have open-ended edges (like the muzzles and tails), join the pieces to the surface of the body by whipstitching all around the open edge to attach them.

### YARN ENDS

It can become pesky business having to deal with attaching, tying off, and sewing in yarn ends when applying embroidery stitches. To make things a bit easier, try this trick. Starting with a new piece of yarn, insert your needle about an inch from where you intend to start your embroidery and leave a 4" tail. Bring the needle up at the first stitch. Hold the yarn tail down with your fingers as you work the first couple of stitches until the yarn appears to feel secure. When you finish your last stitch, bring the needle out at the same spot of the beginning tail and cut the end, leaving another 4" tail. Knot the two yarn tails together, and then use a crochet hook or tapestry needle to draw the yarn and the knot back through the hole. It might take a bit of a tug to pull the knot and yarn tails through, but everything will be nice and hidden.

### EYE OPTIONS

Knowing who the recipient of the toy will be will help you determine which eye option is most suitable.

**Plastic eyes:** Plastic eyes are a great option for children over three years old. A great bonus of using plastic eyes is that you can easily move them around the face (prior to securing the backings) and try different sizes to get a good sense of what will work the best on your toy.

**French knots:** Little embroidered knots add a nice textural element to your toy's face and achieve a look close to that of the plastic eyes, but are a safer option for children under three. See page 16 for instructions on how to make these cute little knots.

**Felt circles:** Eye patterns are on page 76. They match the diameters of the various plastic eyes used in this book. A small pair of sewing scissors or cuticle scissors will make cutting out these little circles easier. If you anticipate making many eyes of the same size, it might be worthwhile to purchase a good-quality hole punch. Attach the felt circles using thread and a running stitch (page 16), or with fabric glue.

Three little penguins sporting different types of eyes: plastic safety eyes, French knots, and felt circles (from left to right)

## Lining Them Up

To ensure the animal's eyes and nose end up in the right spot, look over the finishing illustrations and photos for each toy before you begin assembling them. The illustrations will help you with the final placement of your animal's features, and the projects steps will provide clear instruction regarding spacing.

### CUTTING FELT SHAPES

You can make templates using tracing paper or a photocopier/scanner, or by downloading and printing the patterns from ShopMartingale.com/extras.

### Tracing Paper

The tracing-paper method is best if you only need to cut out one or two pieces for your project. If you need more than two pieces, see "Printer or Copier" on facing page.

## Multiple Pattern Sizes

Several of the patterns are drawn in multiple sizes to make it easier for you to find a patch to fit your project without needing to resize it on a copier.

Place the tracing paper over the pattern and trace the shape onto the paper with a pencil. Loosely cut out the traced pattern leaving about a ¼" border around the shape. Cut out a square of felt large enough to accommodate the pattern. You can use a few straight pins to secure the template to the felt, or using some packing tape, tape the template down so that both the tracing paper and the felt are covered. Proceed to cut out the shape.

You can double up the felt using the taping method if you need two of the same shape, but make sure the tape only folds around the felt stack just enough to hold it together (taking care to not cover the bottom of the second piece of felt with tape). The tape will not be removed easily from the felt once it sticks.

I don't recommend using your best fabric scissors for this method, as the tape will leave a sticky residue on the blades. If you need to clean your scissor blades, a little Goo Gone (sold at craft stores) will take off the tape residue.

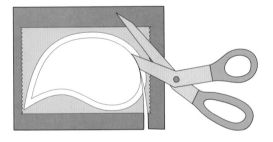

## Tracing Tip

Here's a nifty little trick using Glad Press'n Seal. Unroll a piece large-enough to cover the pattern. Place it tacky side down on top of the pattern, then trace around it with a pencil or pen. Pull the plastic off the paper and stick it onto the felt. Cut out the shape, peel off the plastic wrap, and you're good to go!

**Printer or Copier**

Print the pattern you need using either a computer scanner or a copy machine. You can also resize a pattern easily using this method, if desired. There are several ways to transfer the patterns to the felt. You can also download and print out the various patterns from ShopMartingale.com/extras.

- Cut out the pattern with scissors and trace it onto the felt using either a ballpoint pen or a pencil on light-colored felt and a white gel pen on dark felt.
- Cut out the pattern with scissors leaving a ¼" border and staple it to the felt. Cut out the shape, and then remove the staples. If you need multiples of the same shape, you can stack a few pieces of felt beneath the template.
- Print the pattern onto cardstock and create a stencil by cutting out the shapes using a utility craft knife and a cutting mat. Applying firm pressure, hold the stencil down on top of the felt and carefully cut out the felt shape using the stencil as a guide. This works best when the utility knife has a fresh blade. This is a great method for cutting small, skinny shapes like the tiger stripes.

**DOUBLE THREADING A NEEDLE**

Here's a trick for when you want a little extra thread strength when sewing your felt shapes onto the animals. Cut a piece of thread twice as long as you normally would need for sewing around the shape. Fold the thread in half and insert both ends into the eye of the sewing needle to create a big loop. Pass the needle in and out of the surface of your toy, pulling the thread partially through until there is only a 2" or 3" loop of thread left at the surface of your work. Stop pulling and guide your needle through this small loop. Pull gently to tighten the loop and secure your needle and thread. Once your thread is secured you can then sew on your felt patch with the doubled thread. For kids' toys, I think this method is a bit more robust since they can't easily pull the thread out, and as a bonus, you don't need to knot or tie off the thread at the beginning.

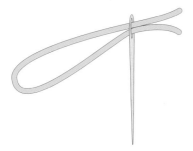

**FRINGE TECHNIQUE**

Use this technique to apply manes and tails to your animals. You'll need your crochet hook and enough pieces of yarn to cover the desired area. It's always better to cut the pieces a little longer and trim them down after they've been applied. To make quick work of cutting the yarn for hair, try winding the yarn around three or four fingers (depending on how long you want the pieces to be), and then cutting all the loops at one time.

❶ To apply a fringe, choose a spot on the toy to add a strand of yarn and insert your crochet hook under that surface stitch. Fold the strand of yarn over your crochet hook and draw it back through the surface of the toy forming a small loop.

❷ Pull the loose ends of the yarn through the loop and pull tightly to knot it.

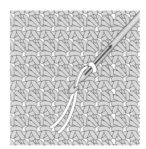

❸ Once the yarn has been applied, use a steel tapestry needle to separate the yarn strands for a fuller look before trimming to the desired length. If you want to go super fluffy, you can also use your pet-slicker brush (page 8) on the separated yarn strands.

For more fur, mane, and hair ideas, check out the "Zookeepers" on page 69.

# Penguins

These cute little guys are quick to make and very simple—so you may want to make a whole colony of them for your zoo! This is a great pattern to start with since the adult and baby penguin pattern pieces will turn up again and again throughout the book as the various animal body parts (like bodies, legs, and ears).

**Skill Level:** Beginner ■□□□   **Finished Size:** Adult: approx 3" tall   Baby: approx 1½" tall

## MATERIALS

**For Adult Penguin**
Worsted-weight yarn in black (approx 20 yds) **4**
6 mm or 7 mm black plastic eyes with safety backings

**For Baby Penguin**
Worsted-weight yarn in fuzzy gray (approx 15 yds) and black (approx 5 yds) **4**
4 mm or 5 mm black plastic eyes with safety backings

**For Both**
DK-weight yarn in orange (5 yds) **3**
Size G-6 (4 mm) crochet hook
6" x 6" square of white craft felt (for adult and baby)
Tapestry needle
Sewing needle and thread
Stuffing
Stitch markers to indicate beginning of rnds (optional)

## Adult Penguin

### BODY

Using black yarn, make an 8-st adjustable ring (page 12).

Rnd 1: Sc 2 in each sc around. (16 sts)

Rnd 2: *Sc 3, sc 2 in next sc; rep from * 3 more times. (20 sts)

Rnd 3: *Sc 1, sc 2 in next sc; rep from * 9 more times. (30 sts)

Rnds 4–8: Sc 30.

Rnd 9: *Sc 1, sc2tog; rep from * 9 more times. (20 sts)

Rnd 10: Sc 20.

Rnd 11: *Sc 3, sc2tog; rep from * 3 more times. (16 sts)

Rnd 12: Sc 16.

Rnd 13: Sc2tog 8 times. (8 sts)
Stuff body.

Rnd 14: *Sc 2, sc2tog; rep from * 1 more time. (6 sts)

Fasten off, leaving a long tail. Close up hole unless using plastic eyes.

### WING (MAKE 2.)

Using black yarn, loosely ch 6. Starting in 2nd ch from hook and working in back ridge loops, sc 2, hdc 2, dc 2 in back ridge loop of next ch. Rotate work. Starting in next ch and working in front loops, hdc 2, sc 2, sl st in next st and fasten off, leaving a long tail.

### FINISHING

❶ Using the appropriately-sized pattern on page 76, cut out adult penguin belly patch from white felt, and sew it to body using running st (page 16). Use pen or pencil to mark where eyes should go. Use sewing needle to make hole where eyes are marked, then a tapestry needle to enlarge hole. Attach plastic eyes and close up 6-st hole on the body using

the yarn tail. If you prefer, you can also use black yarn to make French knots (page 16), or sew on felt circles for eyes.

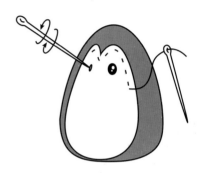

❷ With orange yarn, embroider beak using satin sts (page 16). With black yarn, add eyebrows using a single satin st. Using fringe technique (page 19) and black yarn, cut 3 pieces, 4" long, and attach to top of head. Use tapestry needle to separate yarn strands and trim ends to desired length with scissors.

Trim.

**3** Attach wings to sides of body using the whipstitch (page 17).

**4** To shape the tail, pinch the lower back and bottom to flatten. With black yarn, sew 4 or 5 small running sts in a horizontal line, stitching from the base of penguin up through to the lower back to hold the shape.

# Baby Penguin

## BODY

Using fuzzy gray yarn, make a 6-st adjustable ring.

**Rnd 1:** Sc 3, sc 2 in next sc, sc 3 in next sc, sc 2 in next sc. (10 sts)

**Rnd 2:** Sc 3, *sc 2 in next sc; rep from * 6 more times. (17 sts)

**Rnd 3:** Sc 17 in bl.

**Rnds 4 and 5:** Sc 17.

**Rnd 6:** Sc2tog, *sc 1, sc2tog; rep from * 4 more times. (11 sts)

Change to black yarn.

**Rnd 7:** Sc 1, *sc 3, sc2tog; rep from * 1 more time. (9 sts)

**Rnds 8 and 9:** Sc 9.

Stuff body.

**Rnd 10:** *Sc 1, sc2tog; rep from * 2 more times. (6 sts)

Fasten off, leaving a long tail. Do not close hole if using plastic eyes.

## WING (MAKE 2.)

Using fuzzy gray yarn, make a 9-st adjustable ring. Ch 1 and turn.

Sk first ch, sc 8. (8 sts)

Sl st and fasten off, leaving a long tail for sewing.

## FINISHING

**1** Using pattern on page 76, cut out baby penguin face from white felt and sew it to black portion of body using running st. Use pen or pencil to mark where eyes should go. Refer to steps 1 and 2 in adult finishing to apply eyes (without eyebrows) and beak.

**2** Sew up opening on body and whipstitch wings onto sides of penguin to complete.

# Harp Seals

Who could resist falling in love with this adorable harp seal and her pup! For an extra-fluffy baby harp seal, try using a fuzzy DK- or sport-weight yarn (like mohair or angora) and give him a good brushing all over with your pet slicker brush to loosen up the yarn fibers. Don't forget to check out the fish pattern on page 74 for when it's dinnertime for your seal family. They'll be glad you did!

**Skill Level:** Easy ◼◼☐▱

**Finished Size:** Approx 5" tall and 7" long

## MATERIALS

Worsted-weight yarn in light gray (approx 125 yds) and black (approx 2 yds)
Size G-6 (4 mm) crochet hook
8 mm or 9 mm black plastic eyes with safety backings
Tapestry needle
Stuffing
Stitch markers to indicate beginning of rnds (optional)

## Making the Baby Harp Seal

Follow the pattern as written using DK-weight yarn in white and black, a size D-3 (3.25 mm) or E-4 (3.5 mm) crochet hook, and 6 mm or 7 mm black plastic eyes with safety backings.

### HEAD

Using light-gray yarn, make an 8-st adjustable ring (page 12).
**Rnd 1:** Sc 2 in each sc around. (16 sts)
**Rnd 2:** *Sc 3, sc 2 in next sc; rep from * 3 more times. (20 sts)
**Rnd 3:** *Sc 1, sc 2 in next sc; rep from * 9 more times. (30 sts)
**Rnd 4:** *Sc 4, sc 2 in next sc; rep from * 5 more times. (36 sts)

**Rnds 5–9:** Sc 36.
**Rnd 10:** *Sc 4, sc2tog; rep from * 5 more times. (30 sts)
**Rnd 11:** *Sc 1, sc2tog; rep from * 9 more times. (20 sts)
**Rnd 12:** *Sc 3, sc2tog; rep from * 3 more times. (16 sts)
**Rnd 13:** Sc2tog 8 times. (8 sts)
Stuff head.
**Rnd 14:** *Sc 2, sc2tog; rep from * 1 more time. (6 sts)
Fasten off, leaving a long tail. Close up hole unless using plastic eyes.

### BODY

Using light-gray yarn, make an 8-st adjustable ring.
**Rnd 1:** Sc 2 in each sc around. (16 sts)
**Rnd 2:** *Sc 3, sc 2 in next sc; rep from * 3 more times. (20 sts)
**Rnd 3:** *Sc 1, sc 2 in next sc; rep from * 9 more times. (30 sts)
**Rnds 4–8:** Sc 30.
**Rnd 9:** *Sc 1, sc2tog; rep from * 9 more times. (20 sts)
**Rnd 10:** Sc 20.
**Rnd 11:** *Sc 3, sc2tog; rep from * 3 more times. (16 sts)
**Rnd 12:** Sc 16.

**Rnd 13:** Sc2tog 8 times. (8 sts)
Stuff body.
**Rnd 14:** Sc2tog 4 times. (4 sts)
Fasten off, leaving a long tail. Close up 4-st hole and weave in end.

### FLIPPER (MAKE 4.)

Using light-gray yarn, make a 6-st adjustable ring.
**Rnd 1:** Sc 3, sc 2 in next sc, sc 3 in next sc, sc 2 in next sc. (10 sts)
**Rnd 2:** Sc 3, *sc 2 in next sc; rep from * 6 more times. (17 sts)
**Rnds 3–5:** Sc 17.
**Rnd 6:** Sc2tog, *sc 1, sc2tog; rep from * 4 more times. (11 sts)
**Rnd 7:** Sc 1, *sc 3, sc2tog; rep from * 1 more time. (9 sts)
**Rnd 8:** Sc 9.
**Rnd 9:** Sc 7, sc2tog. (8 sts)
**Rnd 10:** Sc2tog 4 times. (4 sts)
Fasten off, leaving a long tail. Do not stuff.

## MUZZLE

Using light-gray yarn, make an 8-st adjustable ring.

**Rnd 1:** Sc 2 in each sc around. (16 sts)

**Rnd 2:** *Sc 1, sc 2 in next sc; rep from * 7 more times. (24 sts)

**Rnd 3:** Sc 24.

**Rnd 4:** *Sc 1, sc2tog; rep from * 7 more times. (16 sts)

Sl st in next sc and fasten off, leaving a long tail for sewing.

## ASSEMBLY

❶ Attach plastic eyes about 8 rnds from top of head, with 3 sts between them. Close 6-st hole at bottom of head. If you prefer, use black yarn to make French knots (page 16), or sew on felt circles for eyes. Sew on muzzle directly below bottom of eyes. Stuff lightly before closing seam.

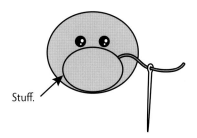

Stuff.

❷ With long strand of black yarn, make lip cleft by pulling yarn through muzzle from back of chin to where bottom of nose will be, then back down to chin and up through muzzle again, pulling tightly to form 2 cheeks. Rep 3 or 4 times. With black yarn, embroider nose using satin st (page 16), and whiskers by making 3 long sts on the side of each cheek. Embroider eyebrows with black yarn using lazy daisy st (page 16).

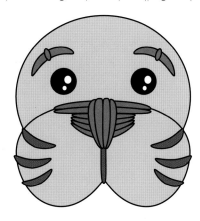

❸ Attach head to body with the larger, rounder end of body facing forward and tilted up slightly. Flatten flippers before attaching them. For front flippers, position one on each side, about 5 rnds

from front and 4 or 5 sts below head. Sew in place. To keep flippers from splaying out, attach yarn to inside surface of one flipper, pass yarn through body to inside surface of opposite flipper, then back again through body to your starting point. Pull yarn gently to draw flippers close to body before fastening off.

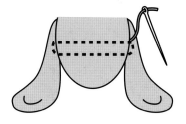

❹ Position back flippers like a fish fin as shown. Sew them to back of body and cover attachment point with 3 or 4 satin sts.

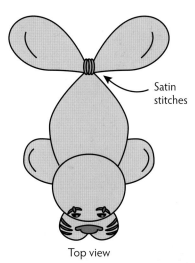

Satin stitches

Top view

# Walrus

Our walrus looks quite dapper with a fine set of whiskers and a stately pair of tusks. When making your walruses, keep in mind that both males and females have whiskers and tusks while your baby walrus will have just a set of cute and fuzzy whiskers.

**Skill Level:** Easy ◼◼◻◻　　**Finished Size:** Approx 5" tall and 7" long

## MATERIALS

Worsted-weight yarn in tawny (approx 125 yds), beige (approx 10 yds), white or ivory (approx 5 yds), and black (approx 2 yds)
Size G-6 (4 mm) crochet hook
8 mm or 9 mm black plastic eyes with safety backings
Tapestry needle
Stuffing
Stitch markers to indicate beginning of rnds (optional)

## HEAD

Using tawny yarn, loosely ch 7.
**Rnd 1:** Starting in 2nd ch from hook and working in back ridge loops, sc 5, sc 8 in back ridge loop of next ch. Rotate work. Starting in next ch and working in front loops, sc 4, sc 7 in front loop of next ch. (24 sts)
**Rnd 2:** Sc 5, *sc 2 in next sc; rep from * 6 more times, sc 5, **sc 2 in next sc; rep from ** 6 more times. (38 sts)
**Rnd 3:** Sc 5, hdc 14, sc 5, hdc 14. (38 sts)
**Rnds 4–6:** Sc 38.
**Rnd 7:** Sc 8, *sc 1, sc2tog; rep from * 9 more times. (28 sts)
**Rnd 8:** Sc 8, sc2tog 5 times, pm, sc2tog 5 times. (18 sts) (The marker will indicate which side of head is the back.)

**Rnds 9–11:** Sc 18.
**Rnd 12:** *Sc 1, sc2tog; rep from * 5 more times. (12 sts)
**Rnd 13:** Sc 12.
**Rnd 14:** *Sc 1, sc2tog; rep from * 3 more times. (8 sts)
Stuff head.
**Rnd 15:** *Sc 2, sc2tog; rep from * 1 more time. (6 sts)
Fasten off, leaving a long tail.
Close up hole unless using plastic eyes.

## BODY

Using tawny yarn, make an 8-st adjustable ring (page 12).
**Rnd 1:** Sc 2 in each sc around. (16 sts)
**Rnd 2:** *Sc 3, sc 2 in next sc; rep from * 3 more times. (20 sts)
**Rnd 3:** *Sc 1, sc 2 in next sc; rep from * 9 more times. (30 sts)
**Rnds 4–8:** Sc 30.
**Rnd 9:** *Sc 1, sc2tog; rep from * 9 more times. (20 sts)
**Rnd 10:** Sc 20.
**Rnd 11:** *Sc 3, sc2tog; rep from * 3 more times. (16 sts)
**Rnd 12:** Sc 16.
**Rnd 13:** Sc2tog 8 times. (8 sts)
Stuff body.
**Rnd 14:** Sc2tog 4 times. (4 sts)
Fasten off, leaving a long tail.
Close up 4-st hole and weave in end.

## FLIPPER (MAKE 4.)

Using tawny yarn, make a 6-st adjustable ring.
**Rnd 1:** Sc 3, sc 2 in next sc, sc 3 in next sc, sc 2 in next sc. (10 sts)
**Rnd 2:** Sc 3, *sc 2 in next sc; rep from * 6 more times. (17 sts)
**Rnds 3–5:** Sc 17.
**Rnd 6:** Sc2tog, *sc 1, sc2tog; rep from * 4 more times. (11 sts)
**Rnd 7:** Sc 1, *sc 3, sc2tog; rep from * 1 more time. (9 sts)
**Rnd 8:** Sc 9.
**Rnd 9:** Sc 7, sc2tog. (8 sts)
**Rnd 10:** Sc2tog 4 times. (4 sts)
Fasten off, leaving a long tail.

## TUSK (MAKE 2.)

Using white or ivory yarn, make a 4-st adjustable ring.
**Rnd 1:** Sc 4 in bl.
**Rnd 2:** *Sc 1, sc 2 in next sc; rep from * 1 more time. (6 sts)
**Rnds 3 and 4:** Sc 6.
Sl st in next sc, and fasten off, leaving a long tail.

## ASSEMBLY

*Side of head that has marker is back of head. Remove marker.*

❶ Attach plastic eyes about 5 or 6 rnds from top of head, with about 2 sts between them. Close 6-st hole at top of head. If you prefer, use black yarn to make French knots (page 16) or sew on felt circles for eyes. With black yarn, make lip cleft by drawing yarn through head from back to front (roughly 6 rnds from bottom of head), then looping yarn under chin and returning to starting point on back of head, pulling tightly to form 2 cheeks. Rep 3 or 4 times.

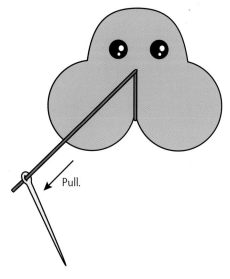

Pull.

❷ With black yarn, embroider nose using satin st (page 16). Embroider eyebrows with black yarn using lazy daisy st (page 16). Attach tusks directly over gaps formed at both ends of foundation ch at bottom of head.

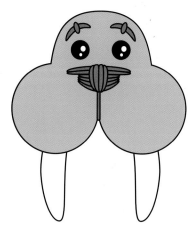

❸ With rounder end of body facing forward and tilted up slightly, attach head using whipstitch (page 17). Flatten flippers before attaching them. For front flippers, position one on each side of body about 5 rnds from center front of body and about 4 or 5 sts below head. Sew them in place.

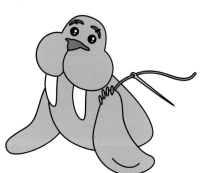

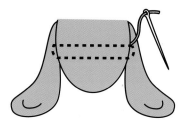

❹ Position back flippers perpendicular to body as shown. Sew them to back of body and cover attachment point with 3 or 4 satin sts.

Satin stitches

Top view

❺ Cut approx 40 pieces of beige yarn, 5" or 6" long, for each cheek. Using fringe technique (page 19), cover fronts of cheeks as indicated in illustration. Separate yarn strands with tapestry needle, and trim to make whiskers.

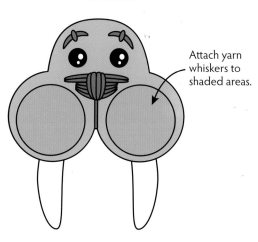

Attach yarn whiskers to shaded areas.

### Whisker Tip

For the walrus whiskers, you can mix things up by crocheting some fun-fur yarn directly to the walrus's cheeks in lieu of using the fringe technique. Check out page 72 for details on how to apply fun-fur yarn to your toys.

# Polar Bear and Grizzly Bear

These friendly bears would be a great addition to anyone's zoo! The grizzly and polar bears share the same pattern. Simply changing the orientation of the head will give you two unique looks!

**Skill Level:** Easy ◼◼☐☐    **Finished Size:** Approx 5" tall and 5" long

## MATERIALS

MC  Worsted-weight yarn in brown for grizzly or white for polar bear (approx 125 yds) ⓵

CC  Worsted-weight yarn in tan for grizzly (approx 25 yds)

Worsted-weight yarn in black (approx 5 yds)

Size G-6 (4 mm) crochet hook

8 mm or 9 mm black plastic eyes with safety backings

Tapestry needle

Stuffing

Stitch markers to indicate beginning of rnds (optional)

## More Bears

If you're in the mood to make a few more bears, try a darker yarn for a black bear or try a smaller gauge [DK-weight or sport-weight yarn and an E-4 (3.5 mm) or D-3 (3.25 mm) hook] for a family of baby bears!

## HEAD

Using MC, loosely ch 7.

**Rnd 1:** Starting in 2nd ch from hook and working in back ridge loops, sc 5, sc 8 in back ridge loop of next ch. Rotate work. Starting in next ch and working in front loops, sc 4, sc 7 in front loop of next ch. (24 sts)

**Rnd 2:** Sc 5, *sc 2 in next sc; rep from * 6 more times, sc 5, **sc 2 in next sc; rep from ** 6 more times. (38 sts)

**Rnd 3:** Sc 5, hdc 14, sc 5, hdc 14. (38 sts)

**Rnds 4–6:** Sc 38.

**Rnd 7:** Sc 8, *sc 1, sc2tog; rep from * 9 more times. (28 sts)

**Rnd 8:** Sc 8, sc2tog 5 times, pm, sc2tog 5 times. (18 sts) (The marker will indicate which side of head is the back.)

**Rnds 9–11:** Sc 18.

**Rnd 12:** *Sc 1, sc2tog; rep from * 5 more times. (12 sts)

**Rnd 13:** Sc 12.

**Rnd 14:** *Sc 1, sc2tog; rep from * 3 more times. (8 sts) Stuff head.

**Rnd 15:** *Sc 2, sc2tog; rep from * 1 more time. (6 sts)

Fasten off, leaving a long tail. Close up hole unless using plastic eyes.

## BODY

Using MC, make an 8-st adjustable ring (page 12).

**Rnd 1:** Sc 2 in each sc around. (16 sts)

**Rnd 2:** *Sc 3, sc 2 in next sc; rep from * 3 more times. (20 sts)

**Rnd 3:** *Sc 1, sc 2 in next sc; rep from * 9 more times. (30 sts)

**Rnds 4–8:** Sc 30.

**Rnd 9:** *Sc 1, sc2tog; rep from * 9 more times. (20 sts)

**Rnd 10:** Sc 20.

**Rnd 11:** *Sc 3, sc2tog; rep from * 3 more times. (16 sts)

**Rnd 12:** Sc 16.

**Rnd 13:** Sc2tog 8 times. (8 sts) Stuff body.

**Rnd 14:** Sc2tog 4 times. (4 sts)

Fasten off, leaving a long tail. Close up 4-st hole and weave in end.

## LEG (MAKE 4.)

Starting with CC *for grizzly* or MC *for polar bear*, make a 6-st adjustable ring.

**Rnd 1:** Sc 3, sc 2 in next sc, sc 3 in next sc, sc 2 in next sc. (10 sts)

**Rnd 2:** Sc 3, *sc 2 in next sc; rep from * 6 more times. (17 sts)

Switch to MC *for grizzly*, cont with MC *for polar bear*.

**Rnd 3:** Sc 17 in bl.

**Rnd 4:** Sc 1, sc2tog 8 times. (9 sts)

**Rnd 5:** Sc 9 in bl.

**Rnds 6–8:** Sc 9.

Stuff leg.

**Rnd 9:** Sc 1, sc2tog 4 times. (5 sts)

Fasten off, leaving a long tail. Close up 5-st hole and weave in end.

## TAIL

Using MC, make a 6-st adjustable ring.

**Rnd 1:** Sc 2 in each sc around. (12 sts)

**Rnds 2 and 3:** Sc 12.

**Rnd 4:** Sc2tog 6 times. (6 sts)

Stuff tail and fasten off, leaving a long tail.

## MUZZLE

Using CC *for grizzly* or MC *for polar bear*, make an 8-st adjustable ring.

**Rnd 1:** Sc 2 in each sc around. (16 sts)

**Rnd 2:** *Sc 1, sc 2 in next st; rep from * 7 more times. (24 sts)

**Rnd 3:** Sc 24.

**Rnd 4:** *Sc 1, sc2tog; rep from * 7 more times. (16 sts)

Fasten off, leaving a long tail.

## EAR (MAKE 2.)

Using MC, make an 8-st adjustable ring. Ch 1 and turn.

Sk first st, sc 8. (8 sts)

Sl st and fasten off, leaving a long tail.

## ASSEMBLY

*For grizzly bear,* orient head so rnd 1 is at top.

*For polar bear,* orient head so rnd 1 is at bottom.

*The side of head that has marker will be back of head. Remove marker before assembly.*

**❶** Attach plastic eyes about 6 rnds from top of head, with 2 sts between them. Close 6-st hole on head. If you prefer, use black yarn to make French knots (page 16), or sew on felt circles for eyes. Attach muzzle directly below bottom of eyes, stuff lightly before closing seam. With black yarn, make a lip cleft by pulling yarn through muzzle from back of chin to where bottom of nose will be, then back down to chin and up through muzzle again, pulling yarn tightly to form 2 cheeks. Rep 3 or 4 times, tying off at chin.

**❷** With black yarn, embroider nose using satin st (page 16), and eyebrows using lazy daisy st (page 16). Attach grizzly bear's ears to top corners of head about 4 rnds above eyes. *For polar bear,* attach ears to sides of head above eye line. Using the fringe technique (page 19) and MC, cut 3 pieces, 4" long, and attach them to top of head. Separate yarn strands with a tapestry needle and trim ends to desired length with scissors.

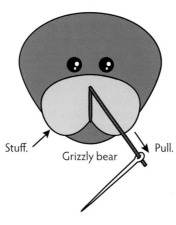

Stuff. Grizzly bear Pull.

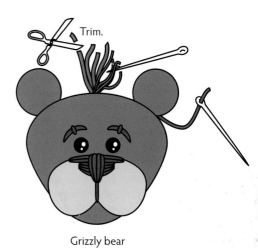

Trim.

Grizzly bear

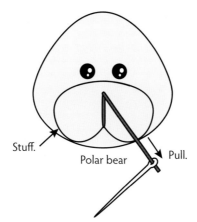

Stuff. Polar bear Pull.

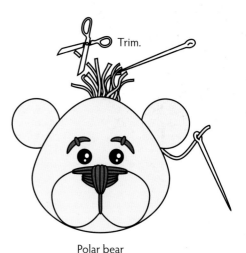

Trim.

Polar bear

**❸** Position body with larger, rounder end of body in back and narrower end in front. Attach head 2 rnds above last rnd of body. Attach legs about halfway up on body. Attach tail.

Grizzly bear

Polar bear

**❹** To keep legs from splaying out, attach yarn to inside surface of one leg, pass yarn through body to inside surface of opposite leg, then back again through body to your starting point. Pull yarn gently to draw legs close to body before fastening off. With black yarn, form toes by looping yarn from rnd 1 around to rnd 5 on leg, and through foot back to rnd 1 again, 2 or 3 times, pulling tightly to form toes. Rep about 3 sts away from first set of loops.

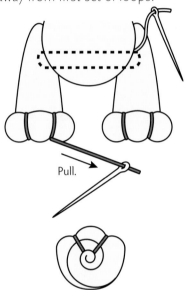

Pull.

Bottom

# Panda

Hailing all the way from China, our round little panda loves to play with his grizzly and polar bear friends, although he might not be so inclined to share his lunch of bamboo. You may notice that his eye patches were inspired by the yin and yang symbol, which literally means dark and light—a fitting detail for this black-and-white panda.

Skill Level: Easy ◼◼◻◻     Finished Size: Approx 5" tall and 5" long

## MATERIALS

MC  Worsted-weight yarn in white (approx 100 yds)
CC  Worsted-weight yarn in black (approx 50 yds)
Size G-6 (4 mm) crochet hook
8 mm or 9 mm black plastic eyes with safety backings
4" x 6" piece of black craft felt
Tapestry needle
Sewing needle and black thread
Stuffing
Stitch markers to indicate beginning of rnds (optional)

## HEAD

Using MC, make an 8-st adjustable ring (page 12).

**Rnd 1:** Sc 2 in each sc around. (16 sts)

**Rnd 2:** *Sc 3, sc 2 in next sc; rep from * 3 more times. (20 sts)

**Rnd 3:** *Sc 1, sc 2 in next sc; rep from * 9 more times. (30 sts)

**Rnd 4:** *Sc 4, sc 2 in next sc; rep from * 5 more times. (36 sts)

**Rnds 5–9:** Sc 36.

**Rnd 10:** *Sc 4, sc2tog; rep from * 5 more times. (30 sts)

**Rnd 11:** *Sc 1, sc2tog; rep from * 9 more times. (20 sts)

**Rnd 12:** *Sc 3, sc2tog; rep from * 3 more times. (16 sts)

**Rnd 13:** Sc2tog 8 times. (8 sts)
Stuff head.

**Rnd 14:** *Sc 2, sc2tog; rep from * 1 more time. (6 sts)

Fasten off, leaving a long tail. Close up hole unless using plastic eyes.

## BODY

Starting with MC, make an 8-st adjustable ring.

**Rnd 1:** Sc 2 in each sc around. (16 sts)

**Rnd 2:** *Sc 3, sc 2 in next sc; rep from * 3 more times. (20 sts)

**Rnd 3:** *Sc 1, sc 2 in next sc; rep from * 9 more times. (30 sts)

**Rnds 4–8:** Sc 30.
Switch to CC.

**Rnd 9:** *Sc 1, sc2tog; rep from * 9 more times. (20 sts)

**Rnd 10:** Sc 20.

**Rnd 11:** *Sc 3, sc2tog; rep from * 3 more times. (16 sts)

**Rnd 12:** Sc 16.

**Rnd 13:** Sc2tog 8 times. (8 sts)
Stuff body.

**Rnd 14:** Sc2tog 4 times. (4 sts)

Fasten off, leaving a long tail. Close up 4-st hole and weave in end.

## LEG (MAKE 4.)

Using CC, make a 6-st adjustable ring.

**Rnd 1:** Sc 3, sc 2 in next sc, sc 3 in next sc, sc 2 in next sc. (10 sts)

**Rnd 2:** Sc 3, *sc 2 in next sc; rep from * 6 more times. (17 sts)

**Rnd 3:** Sc 17 in bl.

**Rnd 4:** Sc 1, sc2tog 8 times. (9 sts)

**Rnd 5:** Sc 9 in bl.

**Rnds 6–8:** Sc 9.
Stuff leg.

**Rnd 9:** Sc 1, sc2tog 4 times. (5 sts)

Fasten off, leaving a long tail. Close up 5-st hole and weave in end.

## TAIL

Using CC, make a 6-st adjustable ring.

**Rnd 1:** Sc 2 in each sc around. (12 sts)

**Rnds 2 and 3:** Sc 12.

**Rnd 4:** Sc2tog 6 times. (6 sts)
Stuff tail.

Fasten off, leaving a long tail for sewing.

## MUZZLE

Using MC, make an 8-st adjustable ring.

**Rnd 1:** Sc 2 in each sc. (16 sts)

**Rnd 2:** *Sc 1, sc 2 in next st; rep from * 7 more times. (24 sts)

**Rnd 3:** Sc 24.

**Rnd 4:** *Sc 1, sc2tog; rep from * 7 more times. (16 sts)

Fasten off, leaving a long tail for sewing.

### EAR (MAKE 2.)

Using CC, make an 8-st adjustable ring. Ch 1 and turn.

Sk first st, sc 8.

Sl st and fasten off, leaving a long tail for sewing.

### ASSEMBLY

❶ Hold the head with the opening facing down. Using pattern on page 76, cut out 2 felt eye patches. If you're attaching plastic eyes, use a sewing needle and then a tapestry needle to enlarge a hole in each felt patch. Insert just the eye posts into patches before applying them to head. The plastic eyes should be 6 or 7 rnds from top of head, with about 3 sts between inside edges of patches. Once plastic eyes and patches are in position, attach safety backings, and sew patches in place with black thread and running st (page 16), taking care to leave a large-enough space between patches for muzzle. Close up hole in head.

If you prefer, use white or light-gray yarn to make French knots (page 16), or sew on white or gray felt circles for eyes. The white or gray will show up on the black patches.

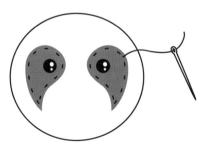

❷ Position muzzle below, between the 2 eye patches. Sew in place, stuffing lightly before closing seam. With black yarn,

make lip cleft by pulling yarn through muzzle from back of chin to where bottom of nose will be, then loop yarn back under chin to starting point, pulling tightly to form 2 cheeks. Rep 3 or 4 times.

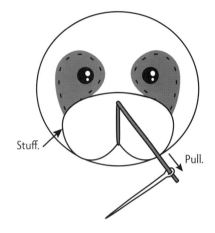

❸ With black yarn, embroider nose using satin st (page 16). With black yarn, embroider eyebrows 1 rnd above eye patches using lazy daisy st (page 16). Attach ears to top of head above eye patches.

❹ Attach head to black end of body. Attach tail. Attach legs about halfway up on body.

❺ To keep legs from splaying out, attach yarn to inside surface of one leg, pass yarn through body to inside surface of opposite leg, then back again through body to your starting point. Pull yarn gently to draw legs close to body before fastening off. Form toes. With MC, insert yarn at rnd 1 and come out at rnd 5 on leg, then through foot back to rnd 1 again, pulling tightly to form toe. Rep 2 or 3 times, pulling tightly each time. Rep one more time 2 or 3 sts away to form next toe.

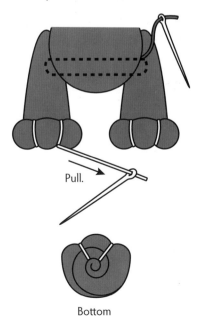

Bottom

# Lion and Tiger

This is the lion that sparked the rest of the animal patterns in this book. This little lion kept my newborn son company during his first night in the hospital after he was born. You can easily make either a male or female lion by adding or omitting the mane. The tiger uses the same pattern as the lion with the addition of stripes and some fuzzy white cheek details.

**Skill Level:** Easy ■■□□       **Finished Size:** Approx 5" tall and 5" long

## MATERIALS

**For Lion**
MC  Worsted-weight yarn in beige (approx 125 yds) 4
CC  Worsted-weight yarn in cream (approx 25 yds)
Worsted-weight yarn in black (approx 5 yds) and orange (approx 25 yds)
6" x 6" piece of cream craft felt

**For Tiger**
MC  Worsted-weight yarn in orange (approx 125 yds) 4
CC  Worsted-weight yarn in ivory (approx 25 yds)
Worsted-weight yarn in black (approx 10 yds) and pink (approx 1 or 2 yds)
6" x 6" piece of ivory craft felt
8½" x 11" piece of black craft felt

**For Both**
Size G-6 (4 mm) crochet hook
8 mm to 9 mm black plastic eyes with safety backings
Tapestry needle
Sewing needle and sewing thread to match felt
Stuffing
Stitch markers to indicate beginning of rnds (optional)

## HEAD

Using MC, loosely ch 7.
**Rnd 1:** Starting in 2nd ch from hook and working in back ridge loops, sc 5, sc 8 in back ridge loop of next ch. Rotate work. Starting in next ch and working in front loops, sc 4, sc 7 in front loop of next ch. (24 sts)
**Rnd 2:** Sc 5, *sc 2 in next sc; rep from * 6 more times, sc 5, **sc 2 in next sc; rep from ** 6 more times. (38 sts)
**Rnd 3:** Sc 5, hdc 14, sc 5, hdc 14. (38 sts)
**Rnds 4–6:** Sc 38.
**Rnd 7:** Sc 8, *sc 1, sc2tog; rep from * 9 more times. (28 sts)
**Rnd 8:** Sc 8, sc2tog 5 times, pm, sc2tog 5 times. (18 sts) (The marker will indicate which side of head is the back.)
**Rnds 9–11:** Sc 18.
**Rnd 12:** *Sc 1, sc2tog; rep from * 5 more times. (12 sts)
**Rnd 13:** Sc 12.
**Rnd 14:** *Sc 1, sc2tog; rep from * 3 more times. (8 sts)
Stuff head.
**Rnd 15:** Sc2tog 2 times. (6 sts)
Fasten off, leaving a long tail. Close up hole unless using plastic eyes.

## BODY

Using MC, make an 8-st adjustable ring (page 12).
**Rnd 1:** Sc 2 in each sc around. (16 sts)
**Rnd 2:** *Sc 3, sc 2 in next sc; rep from * 3 more times. (20 sts)
**Rnd 3:** *Sc 1, sc 2 in next sc; rep from * 9 more times. (30 sts)
**Rnds 4–8:** Sc 30.
**Rnd 9:** *Sc 1, sc2tog; rep from * 9 more times. (20 sts)
**Rnd 10:** Sc 20.
**Rnd 11:** *Sc 3, sc2tog; rep from * 3 more times. (16 sts)
**Rnd 12:** Sc 16.
**Rnd 13:** Sc2tog 8 times. (8 sts)
Stuff body.
**Rnd 14:** Sc2tog 4 times. (4 sts)
Fasten off, leaving a long tail. Close up 4-st hole and weave in end.

## LEG (MAKE 4.)

Starting with CC, make a 6-st adjustable ring.
**Rnd 1:** Sc 3, sc 2 in next sc, sc 3 in next sc, sc 2 in next sc. (10 sts)
**Rnd 2:** Sc 3, *sc 2 in next sc; rep from * 6 more times. (17 sts)
**Rnd 3:** Sc 17 in bl.
**Rnd 4:** Sc 1, sc2tog 8 times. (9 sts)
Switch to MC.
**Rnd 5:** Sc 9 in bl.
**Rnds 6–8:** Sc 9.
Stuff leg.
**Rnd 9:** Sc 1, sc2tog 4 times. (5 sts)
Fasten off, leaving a long tail. Close up 5-st hole and weave in end.

## TAIL

Using MC, make a 6-st adjustable ring.

**Rnd 1:** Sc 2 in each sc around. (12 sts)

**Rnds 2 and 3:** Sc 12.

**Rnd 4:** Sc2tog 6 times. (6 sts)

Stuff and fasten off, leaving a long tail.

## MUZZLE

Using CC, make an 8-st adjustable ring.

**Rnd 1:** Sc 2 in each sc around. (16 sts)

**Rnd 2:** *Sc 1, sc 2 in next st; rep from * 7 more times. (24 sts)

**Rnd 3:** Sc 24.

**Rnd 4:** *Sc 1, sc2tog; rep from * 7 more times. (16 sts)

Fasten off, leaving a long tail.

## EAR (MAKE 2.)

Using MC, loosely ch 6.

Starting in 2nd ch from hook and working in back ridge loops, sc 2, hdc 2, dc 2 in back ridge loop of next ch. Rotate work. Starting in next ch and working in front loops, hdc 2, sc 2, sl st into next st and fasten off, leaving a long tail.

### Mom and Cub

You can easily make a female lion by omitting the mane. Then make a cub (shown on page 80) or two by using DK-weight yarn and a size D-3 (3.25 mm) or E-4 (3.5 mm) crochet hook.

## ASSEMBLY

*The side of head that has the marker will be back of head. Remove marker before assembling.*

❶ Attach plastic eyes, about 5 or 6 rnds from top of head, with 1 or 2 sts between them. Close hole at top of head. If you prefer,

use black yarn to make French knots (page 16), or sew on felt circles for eyes. Attach muzzle 1 rnd below bottom of eyes, stuffing lightly before closing seam. With black yarn, make cheeks by pulling yarn through muzzle from back of chin to where nose will be, then back around under chin and up through muzzle, pulling yarn tightly to form 2 cheeks. Rep 3 or 4 times, ending at chin.

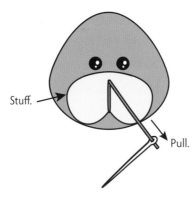

Stuff.

Pull.

❷ *For lion*, use black yarn to embroider the nose using satin st (page 16). *For tiger*, refer to diagram for tiger nose (below) and use pink and black yarn to make nose. For whiskers, use black yarn to make 3 long sts on each side of cheek. Embroider eyebrows using lazy daisy st (page 16). Attach ears above eyes and eyebrows.

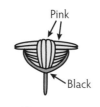

Pink

Black

Tiger nose

❸ With larger, rounder end of body in back, attach head about 2 rnds above last rnd on body. Attach legs about halfway up on body. Attach tail to back end. *For lion only*, using fringe technique (page 19) and orange yarn, cut 8 to 10 pieces, 3" long, and attach to end of tail. Using tapestry needle, separate yarn strands and trim to desired length.

Add fringe to lion only.

Trim.

❹ To keep legs from splaying out, attach yarn to inside surface of one leg, pass yarn through body to inside surface of opposite leg, then back again through body to your starting point. Pull yarn gently to draw legs close to body before fastening off. With black yarn, embroider toes by looping yarn from rnd 1 to rnd 5 (where color changes) on each foot 2 or 3 times, pulling tightly each time. Rep 2 or 3 sts away to form next toe.

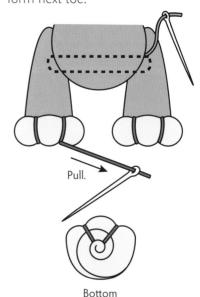

Pull.

Bottom

**5** Using pattern on page 76, cut out 1 belly patch from felt (cream for lion, ivory for tiger) and sew it to body using a running st (page 16).

Bottom

**6** *For mane on adult lion,* using fringe technique, cut approx. 150 pieces, 4" long, of orange yarn and attach them to top and back of head. Separate yarn strands with tapestry needle and trim to desired length.

*For mane on lion cub,* cut 11 pieces, 3" long. Attach 4 each to edge of each check, and remaining 3 to top of head if desired. Use tapestry needle to separate yarn strands and trim to desired length with scissors.

Adult lion

Lion cub

**7** *For tiger,* use tiger stripe patterns on page 76 to cut out stripes from black felt. Sew them to head, body, tail, and legs using illustration for placement reference.

Tiger stripes

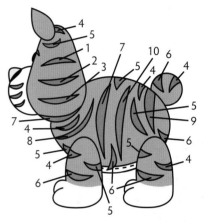

**8** *For fur on tiger,* using fringe technique and white yarn, cut approx 16 pieces, 3" long, and attach 5 to 8 pieces to edge of each cheek. Cut 3 more 3"-long pieces and attach them to top of head. Use tapestry needle to separate yarn strands and trim to desired length.

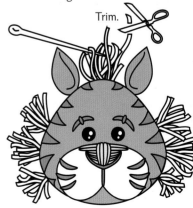

# Rhinoceros

Depending on the species, your rhinoceros can have either one or two horns. If you would like to make a one-horned rhinoceros, simply omit the smaller horn. Or, add an extra third horn for that funky rhino-triceratops look.

**Skill Level:** Easy ◼◼☐☐     **Finished Size:** Approx 5" tall and 5" long

## MATERIALS

Worsted-weight yarn in gray (approx 125 yds), ivory (approx 15 yds), and black (approx 5 yds) 🄴
Size G-6 (4 mm) crochet hook
8 mm or 9 mm black plastic eyes with safety backings
Tapestry needle
Stuffing
Stitch markers to indicate beginning of rnds (optional)

## HEAD

Using gray yarn, make an 8-st adjustable ring (page 12).

**Rnd 1:** Sc 2 in each sc around. (16 sts)

**Rnd 2:** *Sc 3, sc 2 in next sc; rep from * 3 more times. (20 sts)

**Rnds 3–5:** Sc 20.

**Rnd 6:** *Sc 3, sc2tog; rep from * 3 more times. (16 sts)

**Rnd 7:** Sc2tog 8 times. (8 sts)

**Rnd 8:** In fl, *sc 1, sc 2 in next sc; rep from * 3 more times. (12 sts)

**Rnd 9:** In fl, sc 2 in each sc around. (24 sts)

**Rnds 10 and 11:** Sc 24.

**Rnd 12:** Sc2tog 2 times, sc 4, hdc 2, dc 2, pm, dc 2, hdc 2, sc 4, sc2tog 2 times. (20 sts) (The marker will indicate which side of the head should face up.)

**Rnd 13:** Sc2tog, sc 4, hdc 2, dc 4, hdc 2, sc 4, sc2tog. (18 sts)

**Rnd 14:** Sc 5, hdc 2, dc 4, hdc 2, sc 5. (18 sts)

**Rnd 15:** *Sc 4, sc2tog; rep from * 2 more times. (15 sts)

**Rnd 16:** *Sc 3, sc2tog; rep from * 2 more times. (12 sts)

Stuff head.

**Rnd 17:** Sc2tog 6 times. (6 sts)

Fasten off, leaving a long tail. Close up hole unless using plastic eyes.

## BODY

Using gray yarn, make an 8-st adjustable ring.

**Rnd 1:** Sc 2 in each sc around. (16 sts)

**Rnd 2:** *Sc 3, sc 2 in next sc; rep from * 3 more times. (20 sts)

**Rnd 3:** *Sc 1, sc 2 in next sc; rep from * 9 more times. (30 sts)

**Rnds 4–8:** Sc 30.

**Rnd 9:** *Sc 1, sc2tog; rep from * 9 more times. (20 sts)

**Rnd 10:** Sc 20.

**Rnd 11:** *Sc 3, sc2tog; rep from * 3 more times. (16 sts)

**Rnd 12:** Sc 16.

**Rnd 13:** Sc2tog 8 times. (8 sts)

Stuff body.

**Rnd 14:** Sc2tog 4 times. (4 sts)

Fasten off, leaving a long tail. Close up 4-st hole and weave in end.

## LEG (MAKE 4.)

Using gray yarn, make a 6-st adjustable ring.

**Rnd 1:** Sc 3, sc 2 in next sc, sc 3 in next sc, sc 2 in next sc. (10 sts)

**Rnd 2:** Sc 3, *sc 2 in next sc; rep from * 6 more times. (17 sts)

**Rnd 3:** Sc 17 in bl.

**Rnds 4 and 5:** Sc 17.

**Rnd 6:** Sc2tog, *sc 1, sc2tog; rep from * 4 more times. (11 sts)

**Rnd 7:** Sc 1, *sc 3, sc2tog; rep from * 1 more time. (9 sts)

**Rnds 8 and 9:** Sc 9.

Stuff leg.

**Rnd 10:** Sc 1, sc2tog 4 times. (5 sts)

Fasten off, leaving a long tail. Close up 5-st hole and weave in end.

## TAIL

Using gray yarn, make a 6-st adjustable ring.

**Rnd 1:** Sc 2 in each sc around. (12 sts)

**Rnds 2 and 3:** Sc 12.

**Rnd 4:** Sc2tog 6 times. (6 sts)

Stuff and fasten off, leaving a long tail.

## NOSTRIL (MAKE 2.)

Using gray yarn, ch 7.

Starting in 2nd ch from hook, sc in next 6 sc.

Fasten off, leaving a long tail.

## LARGE HORN

Starting with ivory yarn, make a 4-st adjustable ring.

**Rnd 1:** Sc 4 in bl.

**Rnd 2:** *Sc 1, sc 2 in next sc; rep from * 1 more time. (6 sts)

**Rnds 3 and 4:** Sc 6.

Switch to gray yarn.

**Rnd 5:** In fl, sc 2 in each sc around. (12 sts)

**Rnd 6:** Sc2tog 6 times. (6 sts)

Stuff and fasten off, leaving a long tail.

## SMALL HORN

Starting with ivory yarn, make a 4-st adjustable ring.

**Rnd 1:** Sc 4 in bl.

**Rnd 2:** *Sc 1, sc 2 in next sc; rep from * 1 more time. (6 sts)

Switch to gray yarn.

**Rnd 3:** In fl, sc 2 in each sc around. (12 sts)

**Rnd 4:** Sc2tog 6 times. (6 sts)

Stuff and fasten off, leaving a long tail.

## EAR (MAKE 2.)

Using gray yarn, loosely ch 6. Starting in 2nd ch from hook and working in back ridge loops, sc 2, hdc 2, dc 2 in back ridge loop of next ch. Rotate work. Starting in next ch and working in front loops, hdc 2, sc 2, sl st into next st and fasten off, leaving a long tail.

## ASSEMBLY

*When assembling the head, the marker should be facing up. Remove marker before assembly.*

❶ Attach plastic eyes on side of head about 11 rnds from front of head and with 5 sts between them. Close 6-st hole at back of head. If you prefer, use black yarn to make French knots (page 16), or sew on felt circles for eyes. Embroider eyebrows with black yarn using lazy daisy st (page 16).

❷ Sew horns onto bridge of nose, with larger horn in front if your rhinoceros has two horns. Fold nostril piece in half to form a loop and sew ends together to make a

teardrop shape. Sew the nostrils to the front of the head on either side of the front horn.

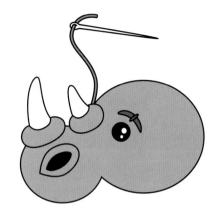

❸ Attach ears 2 rnds above eyebrows. Using fringe technique (page 19), cut 3 pieces of 4"-long black yarn and attach them to top of head. Use tapestry needle to separate yarn strands and trim to desired length.

❹ With larger, rounder end of body in back, attach head 2 rnds above last rnd of body. Attach legs about halfway up on body. Attach tail to back end of body. Using fringe technique and black

yarn, cut 10 to 12 pieces, 3" long, and attach them to end of tail. Using tapestry needle, separate yarn strands and trim to desired length.

⑤ To keep legs from splaying out, attach yarn to inside surface of one leg, pass yarn through body to inside surface of opposite leg, then back again through body to your starting point. Pull yarn gently to draw legs close to body before fastening off. With ivory yarn, embroider 3 toenails using 5 satin sts (page 16) for each nail.

Trim.

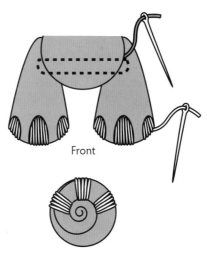

Front

Bottom

# Elephants

Make a whole herd of pachyderms! Elephants are highly social animals, so if you make one, you might want to make at least one more so they can keep each other company.

**Skill Level:** Easy ●■□□

**Finished Size:** Approx 5" tall and 5" long

## Jumbo and Mini Sizes!

You can make your elephant tower over your other zoo animals by using chunky-weight yarn, a size I-9 (5.5 mm) crochet hook, and a pair of 11 mm or 12 mm black plastic eyes with safety backings. To go "mini," stitch your elephant using DK-weight yarn, a size D-3 (3.25 mm) or E-4 (3.5 mm) hook and a set of 6 mm or 7 mm eyes.

## HEAD

Using gray yarn, make an 8-st adjustable ring (page 12).
**Rnd 1:** Sc 8 in bl around.
**Rnds 2–4:** Sc 8.
**Rnd 5:** *Sc 1, sc 2 in next sc; rep from * 3 more times. (12 sts)
**Rnds 6 and 7:** Sc 12.

**Rnds 8–10:** Sc 2, hdc 2, dc 4, hdc 2, sc 2. (12 sts)
**Rnd 11:** In fl, sc 2 in each sc around. (24 sts)
**Rnds 12 and 13:** Sc 24.
**Rnd 14:** Sc2tog 2 times, sc 4, hdc 2, dc 4, hdc 2, sc 4, sc2tog 2 times. (20 sts)
**Rnd 15:** Sc2tog, sc 4, hdc 2, dc 4, hdc 2, sc 4, sc2tog. (18 sts)
**Rnd 16:** Sc 5, hdc 2, dc 4, hdc 2, sc 5. (18 sts)
**Rnd 17:** *Sc 4, sc2tog; rep from * 2 more times. (15 sts)
**Rnd 18:** *Sc 3, sc2tog; rep from * 2 more times. (12 sts)
Stuff head.
**Rnd 19:** Sc2tog 6 times. (6 sts)
Fasten off, leaving a long tail. Close up hole unless using plastic eyes.

## BODY

Using gray yarn, make an 8-st adjustable ring.
**Rnd 1:** Sc 2 in each sc around. (16 sts)
**Rnd 2:** *Sc 3, sc 2 in next sc; rep from * 3 more times. (20 sts)
**Rnd 3:** *Sc 1, sc 2 in next sc; rep from * 9 more times. (30 sts)
**Rnds 4–8:** Sc 30.

**Rnd 9:** *Sc 1, sc2tog; rep from * 9 more times. (20 sts)
**Rnd 10:** Sc 20.
**Rnd 11:** *Sc 3, sc2tog; rep from * 3 more times. (16 sts)
**Rnd 12:** Sc 16.
**Rnd 13:** Sc2tog 8 times. (8 sts)
Stuff body.
**Rnd 14:** Sc2tog 4 times. (4 sts)
Fasten off, leaving a long tail. Close up 4-st hole and weave in end.

## LEG (MAKE 4.)

Using gray yarn, make a 6-st adjustable ring.
**Rnd 1:** Sc 3, sc 2 in next sc, sc 3 in next sc, sc 2 in next sc. (10 sts)
**Rnd 2:** Sc 3, *sc 2 in next sc; rep from * 6 more times. (17 sts)
**Rnd 3:** Sc 17 in bl.
**Rnds 4 and 5:** Sc 17.
**Rnd 6:** Sc2tog, *sc 1, sc2tog; rep from * 4 more times. (11 sts)
**Rnd 7:** Sc 1, *sc 3, sc2tog; rep from * 1 more time. (9 sts)
**Rnds 8 and 9:** Sc 9.
Stuff leg.
**Rnd 10:** Sc 1, sc2tog 4 times. (5 sts)
Fasten off, leaving a long tail. Close up 5-st hole and weave in end.

## TAIL

Using gray yarn, make a 6-st adjustable ring.

**Rnd 1:** Sc 2 in each sc around. (12 sts)

**Rnds 2 and 3:** Sc 12.

**Rnd 4:** Sc2tog 6 times. (6 sts)

Stuff and fasten off, leaving a long tail.

## TUSK (MAKE 2.)

*Both male and female African elephants have tusks, while only the male Asian elephants have a set.*

Using ivory yarn, make a 4-st adjustable ring.

**Rnd 1:** Sc 4 in bl.

**Rnd 2:** *Sc 1, sc 2 in next sc; rep from * 1 more time. (6 sts)

**Rnd 3:** Sc 6.

Switch to gray yarn.

**Rnd 4:** In fl, sc 2 in each sc around. (12 sts)

**Rnd 5:** Sc2tog 6 times. (6 sts)

Stuff and fasten off, leaving a long tail.

## RIGHT EAR

Using gray yarn, make an 8-st adjustable ring.

**Rnd 1:** Sc 2 in each sc around. (16 sts)

**Rnd 2:** *Sc 2 in next sc; rep from * 3 more times, sc 4, **hdc 2 in next sc; rep from ** 2 more times, ***sc 2 in next sc; rep from *** 1 more time, sl st 3. (25 sts)

**Rnd 3:** Sl st 2, sc 2 in next sc, sc 7, hdc 2, *dc 2 in next sc; rep from * 1 more time, hdc 2, sc 3, sl st 5. (27 sts)

Fasten off, leaving a long tail.

## LEFT EAR

Using gray yarn, make an 8-st adjustable ring.

**Rnd 1:** Sc 2 in each sc around. (16 sts)

**Rnd 2:** Sl st 3, *sc 2 in next sc; rep from * 1 more time, **hdc 2 in next sc; rep from ** 2 more times, sc 4, ***sc 2 in next sc; rep from *** 3 more times. (25 sts)

**Rnd 3:** Sl st 5, sc 3, hdc 2, *dc 2 in next sc; rep from * 1 more time, hdc 2, sc 7, sc 2 in next sc, sl st 2. (27 sts)

Fasten off, leaving a long tail.

## ASSEMBLY

① Attach plastic eyes on sides of head about 13 rnds from tip of nose, with 5 or 6 sts between them. Close hole at back of head. If you prefer, use black yarn to make French knots (page 16), or sew on felt circles for eyes. Embroider eyebrows with black yarn using lazy daisy st (page

16). Attach ears to side of head with larger portion of ear hanging down.

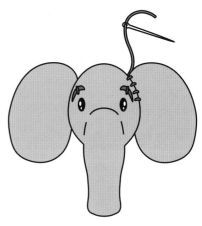

② Attach tusks to sides of trunk where trunk meets head. To keep tusks pointing forward, run a needle and yarn from inside edge of one tusk through trunk to inside edge of other tusk and back again to secure them. Using fringe technique (page 19) and black yarn, cut 3 pieces, 4" long, and attach them to top of head. Use tapestry needle to separate yarn strands and trim to desired length.

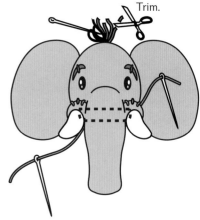

Trim.

③ With larger, rounder end of body in back, attach head 2 rnds above last rnd on body. Attach legs about halfway up on body. Attach tail. Using fringe technique and black yarn, cut 10 to 12 pieces, 3" long, and attach to end of tail.

④ To keep legs from splaying out, attach yarn to inside surface of one leg, pass yarn through body to inside surface of opposite leg, then back again through body to your starting point. Pull yarn gently to draw legs close to body before fastening off. With ivory yarn, embroider 3 toenails using 5 satin sts (page 16) for each nail.

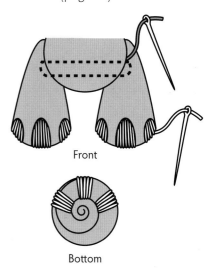

Front

Bottom

Trim.

# Hippopotamus

This portly little hippopotamus loves nothing more than to relax by his pool all day long. You can really play with your hippopotamus's expression by making small adjustments to the eyebrows and eye placement. My son's hippo is done in purple, but you could make yours in gray or blue. Experiment and have fun!

**Skill Level:** Easy ■■□□

**Finished Size:** Approx 5" tall and 5" long

## MATERIALS

Worsted-weight yarn in purple (approx 125 yds), ivory (approx 10 yds), and black (approx 5 yds) (**4**)
Size G-6 (4 mm) crochet hook
8 mm or 9 mm black plastic eyes with safety backings
Tapestry needle
Stuffing
Stitch markers to indicate beginning of rnds (optional)

### HEAD

Using purple yarn, loosely ch 7.

**Rnd 1:** Starting in 2nd ch from hook and working in back ridge loops, sc 5, sc 8 in back ridge loop of next ch. Rotate work. Starting in next ch and working in front loops, sc 4, sc 7 in front loop of next ch. (24 sts)

**Rnd 2:** Sc 5, *sc 2 in next sc; rep from * 6 more times, sc 5, **sc 2 in next sc; rep from ** 6 more times. (38 sts)

**Rnd 3:** Sc 13, hdc 7, sc 4, hdc 7, sc 7. (38 sts)

**Rnds 4–6:** Sc 1 in each sc around. (38 sts)

**Rnd 7:** Sc2tog, *sc 2, sc2tog; rep from * 8 more times. (28 sts)

**Rnd 8:** Sc2tog, *sc 1, sc2tog; rep from * 7 more times, sc2tog. (18 sts)

**Rnd 9:** In fl, sc2tog 9 times. (9 sts)

**Rnd 10:** *Hdc 1, hdc 3 in next st, hdc 1; rep from * 2 more times. (15 sts)

**Rnd 11:** Hdc 1, *hdc 2 in next st, hdc 1; rep from * 6 more times. (22 sts)

**Rnds 12 and 13:** Sc 22.

**Rnd 14:** Sc 1, *sc2tog, sc 1; rep from * 6 more times. (15 sts)

**Rnd 15:** *Sc 1, sc2tog; rep from * 4 more times. (10 sts)

Stuff head.

**Rnd 16:** Sc 2, sc2tog 4 times. (6 sts)

Fasten off, leaving a long tail. Close up hole unless using plastic eyes.

### BODY

Using purple yarn, make an 8-st adjustable ring (page 12).

**Rnd 1:** Sc 2 in each sc around. (16 sts)

**Rnd 2:** *Sc 3, sc 2 in next sc; rep from * 3 more times. (20 sts)

**Rnd 3:** *Sc 1, sc 2 in next sc; rep from * 9 more times. (30 sts)

**Rnds 4–8:** Sc 30.

**Rnd 9:** *Sc 1, sc2tog; rep from * 9 more times. (20 sts)

**Rnd 10:** Sc 20.

**Rnd 11:** *Sc 3, sc2tog; rep from * 3 more times. (16 sts)

**Rnd 12:** Sc 16.

**Rnd 13:** Sc2tog 8 times. (8 sts)

Stuff body.

**Rnd 14:** Sc2tog 4 times. (4 sts)

Fasten off, leaving a long tail. Close up 4-st hole and weave in end.

### LEG (MAKE 4.)

Using purple yarn, make a 6-st adjustable ring.

**Rnd 1:** Sc 3, sc 2 in next sc, sc 3 in next sc, sc 2 in next sc. (10 sts)

**Rnd 2:** Sc 3, *sc 2 in next sc; rep from * 6 more times. (17 sts)

**Rnd 3:** Sc 17 in bl.

**Rnds 4 and 5:** Sc 17.

**Rnd 6:** Sc2tog, *sc 1, sc2tog; rep from * 4 more times. (11 sts)

**Rnd 7:** Sc 1, *sc 3, sc2tog; rep from * 1 more time. (9 sts)

**Rnds 8 and 9:** Sc 9.

Stuff leg.

**Rnd 10:** Sc 1, sc2tog 4 times. (5 sts)

Fasten off, leaving a long tail. Close up 5-st hole and weave in end.

### TAIL

Using purple yarn, make a 6-st adjustable ring.

**Rnd 1:** Sc 2 in each sc around. (12 sts)

**Rnds 2 and 3:** Sc 12.

**Rnd 4:** Sc2tog 6 times. (6 sts)

Stuff and fasten off, leaving a long tail.

## TEETH (MAKE 2.)

Using ivory yarn, make a 5-st adjustable ring.

Sc 1 in each sc. (5 sts)

Fasten off, leaving a long tail.

## EAR (MAKE 2.)

Using purple yarn, loosely ch 6.

Starting in 2nd ch from hook and working in back ridge loops, sc 2, hdc 2, dc 2 in back ridge loop of next ch. Rotate work. Starting in next st and working in front loops of ch, hdc 2, sc 2, sl st into next st and fasten off, leaving a long tail.

## NOSTRIL (MAKE 2.)

Using purple yarn, ch 7.

Starting in 2nd ch from hook, sc in next 6 sc.

Fasten off, leaving a long tail.

## ASSEMBLY

❶ With black yarn, form cheeks by drawing yarn through muzzle from underneath chin up through middle of foundation ch, then back under chin again, pulling yarn tightly to form 2 cheeks. Rep 2 or 3 times, ending underneath chin. Attach plastic eyes, 1 rnd above nose and cheeks, with 2 sts between them. Close hole at back of head. If you prefer, use black

yarn to make French knots (page 16), or sew on felt circles for eyes.

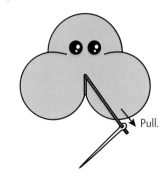

Pull.

❷ With black yarn, embroider eyebrows using lazy daisy st (page 16). Fold nostril piece in half to form a loop and sew ends together to make a teardrop shape. Sew nostrils to front of head over 2 gaps on either side of foundation ch. Sew teeth below nostrils using whipstitch (page 17) so they point straight down.

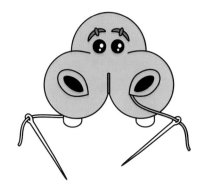

❸ Attach ears above eyes and eyebrows. Using fringe technique (page 19) and black yarn, cut 3 pieces, 4" long, and attach to top of head. Use tapestry needle to separate yarn strands and scissors to trim to desired length.

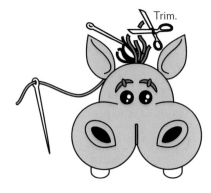

Trim.

❹ With larger, rounder end of body in back, attach head about 2 rnds above last rnd on body. Attach legs about halfway up on body. Attach tail. Using fringe technique and black yarn, cut 8 to 10 pieces, 3" long, and attach to end of tail. Use a tapestry needle to separate yarn strands, and trim to desired length with scissors.

Trim.

❺ To keep legs from splaying out, attach yarn to inside surface of one leg, pass yarn through body to inside surface of opposite leg, then back again through body to your starting point. Pull yarn gently to draw legs close to body before fastening off. With ivory yarn, embroider 3 toenails using 5 satin sts (page 16) for each nail.

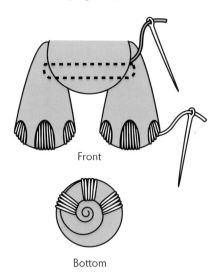

Front

Bottom

# Zebra

This zebra looks quite dashing in his stripes. Although the process of sewing on the stripes can be a bit time consuming, the look of the felt stripes is worth the effort. Don't feel limited to black stripes. Go crazy and try some fun colors for the stripes too!

**Skill Level:** Easy ◼◼◻◻     **Finished Size:** Approx 5" tall and 5" long

## MATERIALS

MC   Worsted-weight yarn in white (approx 125 yds) [4]
CC   Worsted-weight yarn in black (approx 50 yds)
Size G-6 (4 mm) crochet hook
8 mm or 9 mm black plastic eyes with safety backings
8½" x 11" piece of black craft felt
Tapestry needle
Sewing needle and black thread
Stuffing
Stitch markers to indicate beginning of rnds (optional)

## HEAD

Starting with CC, make an 8-st adjustable ring (page 12).

**Rnd 1:** Sc 2 in each sc around. (16 sts)

**Rnds 2–4:** Sc 16.

**Rnd 5:** *Sc 2, sc2tog; rep from * 3 more times. (12 sts)

**Rnd 6:** Sc2tog 6 times. (6 sts)
Switch to MC.

**Rnd 7:** In fl, sc 2 in each sc around. (12 sts)

**Rnd 8:** *Sc 2, sc 2 in next sc; rep from * 3 more times. (16 sts)

**Rnd 9:** *Sc 3, sc 2 in next sc; rep from * 3 more times. (20 sts)

**Rnds 10 and 11:** Sc 20.

**Rnd 12:** *Sc 3, sc2tog; rep from * 3 more times. (16 sts)

**Rnd 13:** *Sc 2, sc2tog; rep from * 3 more times. (12 sts)

**Rnds 14 and 15:** Sc 12.
Stuff head.

**Rnd 16:** Sc2tog 6 times. (6 sts)
Fasten off, leaving a long tail. Close up hole unless using plastic eyes.

## BODY

Using MC, make an 8-st adjustable ring.

**Rnd 1:** Sc 2 in each sc around. (16 sts)

**Rnd 2:** *Sc 3, sc 2 in next sc; rep from * 3 more times. (20 sts)

**Rnd 3:** *Sc 1, sc 2 in next sc; rep from * 9 more times. (30 sts)

**Rnds 4–8:** Sc 30.

**Rnd 9:** *Sc 1, sc2tog; rep from * 9 more times. (20 sts)

**Rnd 10:** Sc 20.

**Rnd 11:** *Sc 3, sc2tog; rep from * 3 more times. (16 sts)

**Rnd 12:** Sc 16.

**Rnd 13:** Sc2tog 8 times. (8 sts)
Stuff body.

**Rnd 14:** Sc2tog 4 times. (4 sts)
Fasten off, leaving a long tail. Close up 4-st hole and weave in end.

## LEG (MAKE 4.)

Starting with CC, make a 6-st adjustable ring.

**Rnd 1:** Sc 3, sc 2 in next sc, sc 3 in next sc, sc 2 in next sc. (10 sts)

**Rnd 2:** Sc 3, *sc 2 in next sc; rep from * 6 more times. (17 sts)

**Rnd 3:** In bl, sc 17.

**Rnds 4 and 5:** Sc 17.
Change to MC.

**Rnd 6:** In bl, sc 1, sc2tog 8 times. (9 sts)

**Rnds 7–10:** Sc 9.
Stuff leg.

**Rnd 11:** Sc 1, sc2tog 4 times. (5 sts)
Fasten off, leaving a long tail. Close up 5-st hole and weave in end.

## TAIL

Using MC, make a 6-st adjustable ring.

**Rnd 1:** Sc 2 in each sc around. (12 sts)

**Rnds 2 and 3:** Sc 12.

**Rnd 4:** Sc2tog 6 times. (6 sts)
Stuff and fasten off, leaving a long tail.

### EAR (MAKE 2.)

Using MC, loosely ch 6.

Starting in 2nd ch from hook and working in back ridge loops, sc 2, hdc 2, dc 2 in back ridge loop of next ch. Rotate work. Starting in next ch and working in front loops, hdc 2, sc 2, sl st into next st and fasten off, leaving a long tail.

### NOSTRIL (MAKE 2.)

Using CC, ch 7.

Starting in 2nd ch from hook, sc 6.

Fasten off, leaving a long tail.

### ASSEMBLY

❶ Attach plastic eyes on sides of head about 11 rnds from front of nose, with 7 sts between them. Close hole at back of head. If you prefer, use black yarn to make French knots (page 16), or sew on felt circles for eyes. With black yarn, embroider eyebrows using lazy daisy st (page 16). Attach ears above eyes and eyebrows. Fold nostril piece in half to form a loop, and sew ends together to make a teardrop shape. Sew nostrils to front of muzzle.

❷ With larger, rounder end of body in back, attach head 2 rnds above last rnd of body. Attach legs about halfway up on body. Attach tail.

❸ Using zebra stripe patterns on page 77, cut felt stripes for face, body, tail, and legs. Following placement diagram, pin stripes in place. Face stripes will start out long and should be trimmed to fit. Use a sewing needle, black thread, and running st (page 16) to attach stripes. Using the fringe technique (page 19) and black yarn, cut approx 30 to 40 pieces, 4" long, and attach to top of head and down back to form mane. Cut 8 to 10 pieces, 3" long, and attach to end of tail. Using tapestry needle, separate yarn strands and trim to desired length.

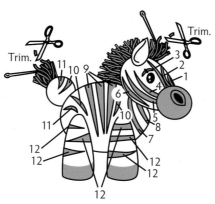

❹ To keep legs from splaying out, attach yarn to inside surface of one leg, pass yarn through body to inside surface of opposite leg, then back again through body to your starting point. Pull yarn gently to draw legs close to body before fastening off. With black yarn, form hooves by inserting yarn through bottom of hoof and out through back of hoof 2 or 3 times, pulling tightly each time needle exits back of hoof.

Front

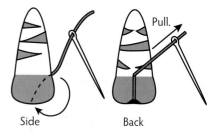

Side          Back

# Giraffe

The sky's the limit with this giraffe. Feel free to make the neck as long as you like! Just remember to make a few extra spots if you do.

**Skill Level:** Easy ◼◼◻◻

**Finished Size:** Approx 10" tall and 5" long

## HEAD

Starting with ivory yarn, make an 8-st adjustable ring (page 12).

**Rnd 1:** Sc 2 in each sc around. (16 sts)

**Rnd 2:** *Sc 3, sc 2 in next sc; rep from * 3 more times. (20 sts)

**Rnds 3–5:** Sc 20.

**Rnd 6:** *Sc 3, sc2tog; rep from * 3 more times. (16 sts)

**Rnd 7:** Sc2tog 8 times. (8 sts)

**Rnd 8:** With yellow, in fl, sc 2 in next sc; with ivory, in fl, *sc 2 in next sc; rep from * 6 more times. (16 sts)

**Rnd 9:** With yellow, sc 2; with ivory, sc 14. (16 sts)

**Rnd 10:** With yellow, *sc 2 in next sc; rep from * 1 more time; with ivory, sc 14. (18 sts)

**Rnd 11:** With yellow, sc 4; with ivory, sc 14. (18 sts)

**Rnd 12:** With yellow, *sc 2 in next sc; rep from * 3 more times; with ivory, sc 14. (22 sts)

**Rnd 13:** With yellow, sc 8; with ivory, sc 14. (22 sts)

Cont with yellow only.

**Rnd 14:** Sc 22.

**Rnd 15:** Sc 3, *sc 2 in next sc; rep from * 1 more time, sc 17. (24 sts)

**Rnd 16:** Sc2tog 12 times. (12 sts) Stuff head.

**Rnd 17:** Sc2tog 6 times. (6 sts)

Fasten off, leaving a long tail. Close up hole unless using plastic eyes.

## BODY AND NECK

Using yellow yarn, make an 8-st adjustable ring.

**Rnd 1:** Sc 2 in each sc around. (16 sts)

**Rnd 2:** *Sc 3, sc 2 in next sc; rep from * 3 more times. (20 sts)

**Rnd 3:** *Sc 1, sc 2 in next sc; rep from * 9 more times. (30 sts)

**Rnds 4–8:** Sc 30.

**Rnd 9:** *Sc 1, sc2tog; rep from * 9 more times. (20 sts)

**Rnd 10:** Sc 20.

**Rnd 11:** Dc 5, *sc 3, sc2tog; rep from * 2 more times. (17 sts)

**Rnd 12:** Dc 6, sc 3, sc2tog, sl st 1, sc2tog, sc 3. (15 sts)

**Rnds 13–15:** Dc 6, sl st 9 in fl. (15 sts)

**Rnds 16 and 17:** Sc 15.

**Rnd 18:** *Sc 3, sc2tog; rep from * 2 more times. (12 sts)

**Rnds 19–29:** Sc 12. (Work additional rnds to make neck longer if you like.)

Stuff and leave neck open for assembly.

## LEG (MAKE 4.)

Starting with brown yarn, make a 6-st adjustable ring.

**Rnd 1:** Sc 3, sc 2 in next sc, sc 3 in next sc, sc 2 in next sc. (10 sts)

**Rnd 2:** Sc 3, *sc 2 in next sc; rep from * 6 more times. (17 sts)

**Rnd 3:** Sc 17 in bl.

**Rnds 4 and 5:** Sc 17.

Change to yellow yarn.

**Rnd 6:** In bl, sc 1, sc2tog 8 times. (9 sts)

**Rnds 7–10:** Sc 9.

Stuff leg.

**Rnd 11:** Sc 1, sc2tog 4 times. (5 sts)

Fasten off, leaving a long tail. Close up 5-st hole and weave in end.

### HORN (MAKE 2.)

Using brown yarn, make a 3-st adjustable ring.

**Rnd 1:** Sc 3.

**Rnd 2:** Sc 2 in fl of each sc around. (6 sts)

Fasten off, leaving a long tail.

### TAIL

Using yellow yarn, make a 6-st adjustable ring.

**Rnd 1:** Sc 2 in each sc around. (12 sts)

**Rnds 2 and 3:** Sc 12.

**Rnd 4:** Sc2tog 6 times. (6 sts)

Stuff and fasten off, leaving a long tail.

### EAR (MAKE 2.)

Using yellow yarn, loosely ch 6. Starting in 2nd ch from hook and working in back ridge loops, sc 2, hdc 2, dc 2 in back ridge loop of next ch. Rotate work. Starting in next ch and working in front loops, hdc 2, sc 2, sl st into next st and fasten off, leaving a long tail.

### NOSTRIL (MAKE 2.)

Using yellow yarn, ch 7. Starting in 2nd ch from hook, sc 6.

Fasten off, leaving a long tail.

### ASSEMBLY

**①** Attach plastic eyes on sides of head about 10 or 11 rnds from nose, with 7 sts between them. Close hole at back of head. If you prefer, use black yarn to make French knots (page 16), or sew on felt circles for eyes. With black yarn, embroider eyebrows above eyes using lazy daisy st (page 16). Fold nostril in half to form a loop and sew ends tog to make a teardrop shape. Sew nostrils to front of head. Attach ears above eyes and eyebrows. Attach horns between ears, leaving room in middle for mane.

**②** Attach head to top of neck. Attach legs about halfway up on body. Using fringe technique (page 19) and black yarn, cut 8 to 10 pieces, 3" long, and attach to end of tail. Cut about 150 pieces, 4" long, and attach to top of head starting between horns and down back of neck to form mane. Use tapestry needle to separate yarn strands and trim to desired length with scissors.

**③** Using belly patch pattern to fit (page 76), cut 1 from ivory felt. With sewing needle and ivory thread, sew belly underneath body between legs using running st (page 16).

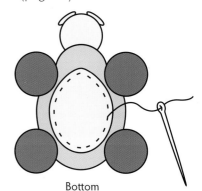

Bottom

④ Using spot patterns (page 77), cut 2 or 3 large spots, 5 to 10 medium spots, and 30 small spots. Referring to illustration and photo, pin large spots on body first; then place medium spots on body and up the remaining neck. Fill in spaces with progressively smaller spots. Pin 2 or 3 small spots to each leg. Feel free to play with the arrangement of spots until your giraffe looks perfect. Using sewing needle and brown thread, sew spots in place using running st.

⑤ To keep legs from splaying out, attach yarn to inside surface of one leg, pass yarn through body to inside surface of opposite leg, then back again through body to your starting point. Pull yarn gently to draw legs close to body before fastening off. With black yarn, shape hooves by inserting needle and yarn through bottom of hoof and out through back of hoof 2 or 3 times, pulling tightly each time needle exits back of hoof.

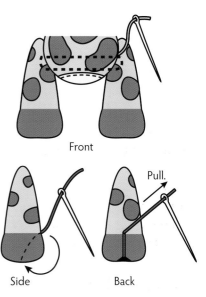

Front

Side

Back

Pull.

# Primates

Gorillas, baboons, and chimpanzees—oh my! This cheeky trio of apes uses the same body patterns, but different head shapes. Let your imagination run wild and try out other color combinations and yarn weights to make all your favorite monkeys. Check out the bonus box on page 64 to make a long tail. And don't forget the bananas (page 75)!

**Skill Level:** Intermediate ■■■□     **Finished Size:** Approx 5" tall and 5" long  (Chimp 4" tall and 4" long)

## MATERIALS

### For Gorilla
MC   Worsted-weight yarn in black (approx 125 yds) [4]
CC   Worsted-weight yarn in gray (approx 25 yds)
Size G-6 (4 mm) crochet hook
8 mm or 9 mm black plastic eyes with safety backings
Small piece of gray craft felt

### For Baboon
MC   Worsted-weight yarn in grayish brown (approx 125 yds) [4]
CC   Worsted-weight yarn in brownish orange (approx 25 yds)
Worsted-weight yarn in light blue (approx 10 yds), medium blue (approx 10 yds), dark blue (approx 10 yds), ivory (approx 15 yds), and red (approx 10 yds)
Size G-6 (4 mm) crochet hook
8 mm or 9 mm black plastic eyes with safety backings

2" x 2" piece of blue craft felt and 4" x 4" piece of tan craft felt

### For Chimpanzee*
MC   DK-weight yarn in black (approx 125 yds) [3]
CC   DK-weight yarn in beige (approx 25 yds)
Size E-4 (3.5 mm) crochet hook
6 mm or 7 mm black plastic eyes with safety backings
Small piece of beige craft felt
*If you'd like to make a larger chimp, use worsted-weight yarn, a G-6 (4 mm) hook, and 8 or 9 mm plastic eyes.

### For All
Tapestry needle
Sewing needle and thread to match felt
Stuffing
Stitch markers to indicate beginning of rnds (optional)

## HEADS
*Each primate has a different-shaped head.*

### Gorilla Head
Using MC, loosely ch 7.

**Rnd 1:** Starting in 2nd ch from hook and working in back ridge loops, sc 5, sc 8 in back ridge loop of next ch. Rotate work. Starting in next ch and working in front loops, sc 4, sc 7 in front loop of next ch. (24 sts)

**Rnd 2:** Sc 5, *sc 2 in next sc; rep from * 6 more times, sc 5, **sc 2 in next sc; rep from ** 6 more times. (38 sts)

**Rnd 3:** Sc 5, hdc 14, sc 5, hdc 14. (38 sts)

**Rnds 4–6:** Sc 38.

**Rnd 7:** Sc 8, *sc 1, sc2tog; rep from * 9 more times. (28 sts)

**Rnd 8:** Sc 8, sc2tog 5 times, pm, sc2tog 5 times. (18 sts) (The marker will indicate which side of head is the back.)

**Rnds 9–11:** Sc 18.

**Rnd 12:** *Sc 1, sc2tog; rep from * 5 more times. (12 sts)

**Rnd 13:** Sc 12.

**Rnd 14:** *Sc 1, sc2tog; rep from * 3 more times. (8 sts)

Stuff head.

**Rnd 15:** *Sc 2, sc2tog; rep from * 1 more time. (6 sts)

Fasten off, leaving a long tail. Close up hole unless using plastic eyes.

## Baboon Head

Using MC, make an 8-st adjustable ring (page 12).

**Rnd 1:** Sc 2 in each sc around. (16 sts)

**Rnd 2:** *Sc 3, sc 2 in next sc; rep from * 3 more times. (20 sts)

**Rnd 3:** *Sc 1, sc 2 in next sc; rep from * 9 more times. (30 sts)

**Rnds 4–8:** Sc 30.

**Rnd 9:** *Sc 1, sc2tog; rep from * 9 more times. (20 sts)

**Rnd 10:** Sc 20.

**Rnd 11:** *Sc 3, sc2tog; rep from * 3 more times. (16 sts)

**Rnd 12:** Sc 16.

**Rnd 13:** Sc2tog 8 times. (8 sts) Stuff body.

**Rnd 14:** *Sc 2, sc2tog; rep from * 1 more time. (6 sts)

Fasten off, leaving a long tail. Close up hole unless using plastic eyes.

## Chimpanzee Head

Using MC, make an 8-st adjustable ring.

**Rnd 1:** Sc 2 in each sc around. (16 sts)

**Rnd 2:** *Sc 3, sc 2 in next sc; rep from * 3 more times. (20 sts)

**Rnd 3:** *Sc 1, sc 2 in next sc; rep from * 9 more times. (30 sts)

**Rnd 4:** *Sc 4, sc 2 in next sc; rep from * 5 more times. (36 sts)

**Rnds 5–9:** Sc 36.

**Rnd 10:** *Sc 4, sc2tog; rep from * 5 more times. (30 sts)

**Rnd 11:** *Sc 1, sc2tog; rep from * 9 more times. (20 sts)

**Rnd 12:** *Sc 3, sc2tog; rep from * 3 more times. (16 sts)

**Rnd 13:** Sc2tog 8 times. (8 sts) Stuff head.

**Rnd 14:** *Sc 2, sc2tog; rep from * 1 more time. (6 sts)

Fasten off, leaving a long tail. Close up hole unless using plastic eyes.

## BODY

Using MC, make an 8-st adjustable ring.

**Rnd 1:** Sc 2 in each sc around. (16 sts)

**Rnd 2:** *Sc 3, sc 2 in next sc; rep from * 3 more times. (20 sts)

**Rnd 3:** *Sc 1, sc 2 in next sc; rep from * 9 more times. (30 sts)

**Rnds 4–8:** Sc 30.

**Rnd 9:** *Sc 1, sc2tog; rep from * 9 more times. (20 sts)

**Rnd 10:** Sc 20.

**Rnd 11:** *Sc 3, sc2tog; rep from * 3 more times. (16 sts)

**Rnd 12:** Sc 16.

**Rnd 13:** Sc2tog 8 times. (8 sts) Stuff body.

**Rnd 14:** Sc2tog 4 times. (4 sts)

Fasten off, leaving a long tail. Close up 4-st hole and weave in end.

## ARM (MAKE 2.)

Starting with CC, make a 6-st adjustable ring.

**Rnd 1:** Sc 3, sc 2 in next sc, sc 3 in next sc, sc 2 in next sc. (10 sts)

**Rnd 2:** Sc 3, *sc 2 in next sc; rep from * 6 more times. (17 sts)

**Rnds 3 and 4:** Sc 17.

Switch to MC.

**Rnd 5:** Sc 1, sc2tog 8 times. (9 sts)

**Rnds 6–8:** Sc 9.

**Rnd 9:** *Sc 2, sc 2 in next sc; rep from * 2 more times. (12 sts)

**Rnds 10–12:** Sc 12.

**Rnd 13:** *Sc 2, sc2tog; rep from * 2 more times. (9 sts)

**Rnd 14:** Sc 9. Stuff arm.

**Rnd 15:** Sc 1, sc2tog 4 times. (5 sts)

Fasten off, leaving long tail.

## LEG (MAKE 2.)

Starting with CC, make a 6-st adjustable ring.

**Rnd 1:** Sc 3, hdc, dc, hdc. (6 sts)

**Rnd 2:** Sc 3, sc 2 in next sc, sc 3 in next sc, sc 2 in next sc. (10 sts)

Switch to MC.

**Rnd 3:** Sc 10 in bl.

**Rnd 4:** *Sc 3, sc2tog; rep from * 1 more time. (8 sts)

**Rnds 5–8:** Sc 8. Stuff leg.

**Rnd 9:** Sc2tog 4 times. (4 sts)

Fasten off, leaving a long tail.

## BIG TOE/THUMB (MAKE 4.)

Using CC, ch 6. Starting in 2nd ch from hook, sc 5.

Fasten off, leaving a long tail.

## FOOT PAD (MAKE 2.)

Using CC, make a 6-st adjustable ring. Ch 1 and turn.

Sk first ch, sc, hdc, dc, hdc, sc, sl st and fasten off, leaving a long tail.

## BROW

Using MC *for gorilla*, light blue *for baboon*, and CC *for chimp*, ch 15.

**Row 1:** Starting in 2nd ch from hook, sc 14, ch 1, turn.

**Rows 2–4:** Sk first ch, sc 14, ch 1, turn.

Fasten off, leaving a long tail. Fold piece in half the long way. Using a whipstitch, sew tog row 1 and row 4 to form a tube.

## MUZZLE AND FACE

Using CC, make an 8-st adjustable ring.

**Rnd 1:** Sc 2 in each sc around. (16 sts)

**Rnd 2:** *Sc 1, sc 2 in next sc; rep from * 7 more times. (24 sts)

**Rnd 3:** Sc 24.

**Rnd 4:** *Sc 1, sc2tog; rep from * 7 more times. (16 sts)

*For baboon only*, switch to dark-blue yarn.

**Row 5:** In bl, sc 1, hdc 6, sc 1, ch 1, turn.

**Rows 6 and 7:** Sk first ch, sc 8, ch 1, turn.

**Row 8:** Sk first ch, sc2tog, sc 1, sc2tog, sc 1, sc2tog, ch 1, turn.

**Row 9:** Sk first ch, sc2tog, sc 1, sc2tog.

Fasten off, leaving a long tail.

## NOSTRIL (MAKE 2.)

Using CC *for gorilla and chimp*, and red yarn *for baboon*, ch 7.

Starting in 2nd ch from hook, sc 6.

Fasten off, leaving a long tail.

## EAR (MAKE 2.)

Using CC, make an 8-st adjustable ring. Ch 1, turn.

Sk first st, sc 8.

Sl st and fasten off, leaving a long tail.

## BABOON TAIL

Using grayish-brown yarn, make a 6-st adjustable ring.

**Rnd 1:** Sc 2 in each sc around. (12 sts)

**Rnds 2 and 3:** Sc 12.

**Rnd 4:** Sc2tog 6 times. (6 sts)

Fasten off, leaving a long tail.

## ASSEMBLY

*For gorilla, orient head with last rnd at top of head, yarn tail side up. The side of head with marker will be back of head. Remove marker before assembling.*

**❶** If you wish to use French knots (page 16) or felt circles for eyes, attach them to face area above muzzle. Attach muzzle and face area to head. Face area should be sewn flat against head. Sew around perimeter of muzzle and stuff before closing up seam. If using plastic eyes, install them now, 1 rnd above top of muzzle with 2 sts between them. Fold nostril piece in half to form a loop and sew ends tog to make a teardrop shape. Attach nostrils to center of muzzle with nostril corners close tog. Pull inside corners of nostrils even closer tog with 2 or 3 additional sts.

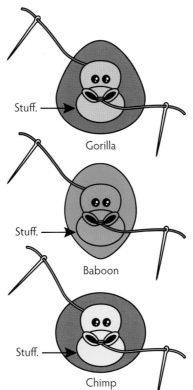

Stuff.

Gorilla

Stuff.

Baboon

Stuff.

Chimp

**❷** Using CC *for chimp and gorilla*, and red yarn *for baboon*, add nose bridge. Beg by embroidering 4 long satin sts (page 16) where bridge of nose will go, starting between nostrils up to space directly below eyes. To build up shape, start at top of bridge and using a satin st, loop yarn over these 4 sts then under the 4 sts and through top of muzzle as many times as it takes to build nose bridge all the way down to nostrils.

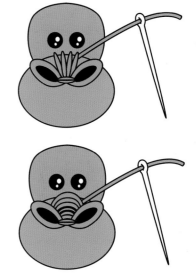

*For baboon* cheeks, use medium-blue yarn and satin sts to fill in space between bridge of nose and top of nostrils. Once areas have been filled in, switch to dark blue and carefully layer 3 dark-blue stitches across surface of each medium-blue cheek to complete look.

**3** Using needle and yarn, attach brow around outside edge of face area. To shape brow, pull yarn over center of brow ridge, through head to a point under chin, and back up to center of brow ridge 2 or 3 times, pulling firmly each time to create 2 distinct eyebrow shapes. Attach ears to sides of head.

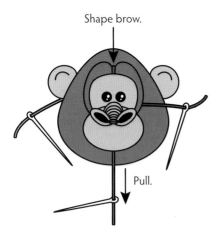

Shape brow.

Pull.

**4** *For gorilla*, using black yarn, cut 4 pieces, 4" long, and use fringe technique (page 19) to attach to top of head. *For baboon*, using ivory yarn, cut 30 pieces, 3" long, and attach all the way around edge of muzzle and sides of face area. Using MC, cut 4 pieces, 3" long, and attach to top of head. *For chimp*, using black yarn, cut 20 pieces, 3" long, and attach to sides of cheeks as well as top of head. Use tapestry needle to

separate yarn strands, and cut to desired length with scissors.

Trim.

Gorilla

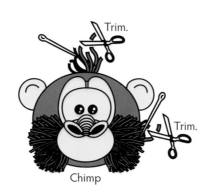

Trim.

Trim.

Baboon

Trim.

Trim.

Chimp

**5** For arm shaping, fold hand portion of arm backward to form a fist and sew in place with CC. Attach a thumb to inside edge of each hand. Attach foot pad to front edge of each leg. Attach big toe to inside edge of each foot.

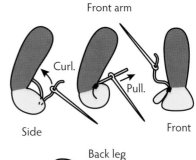

Front arm

Curl.

Pull.

Side

Front

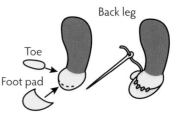

Back leg

Toe

Foot pad

**6** Attach head to larger, rounder end of body. Attach arms 1 or 2 rnds below head. Attach legs. *For baboon only*, sew on tail. To keep arms and legs from splaying out, attach yarn to inside surface of one limb, pass yarn through body to inside surface of opposite limb, then back again through body to your starting point. Pull yarn gently to draw arms and legs close to body before fastening off.

Front

**7** Using felt and heart-patch pattern on page 76 to fit your primate, cut gray heart *for gorilla*, blue heart *for baboon*, and beige heart *for chimp*, and sew to bottom end of body. *For baboon, using belly patch pattern on page 76, cut out 1 tan belly patch and attach to stomach of baboon using running st (page 16).*

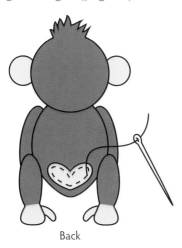

Back

Are you a fan of the majestic golden lion tamarin or perhaps the lovable squirrel monkey? Then you are in luck! With a little imagination, you can mix and match your favorite primate patterns with your monkey's custom colors to make your favorite monkey. For the golden lion tamarin, use the gorilla head and turn it upside down. For the squirrel monkey, use the chimpanzee head. If your monkey is in need of a long tail, we've got you covered.

### Long Monkey Tail

Using MC, make a 5-st adjustable ring.

Sc in each sc around and around until tail is 2 times length of monkey body, or to desired length.

To finish, sc 2 in next sc, sc 1, sc 2 in next sc, sc 1, sc 2 in next sc, and fasten off, leaving a long yarn tail. (8 sts)

Sew tail on last rnd of monkey's body.

For monkey variations, use DK-weight yarn and size D-3 (3.25 mm) or E-4 (3.5 mm) crochet hook. Customize your monkey by adding extra details like hair fringe, a heart patch on the bottom, or switch up the colors as you work through the pattern to create striped effects.

# Giant Red Kangaroo and Joey

This kangaroo has a little surprise in her pouch—a bouncing baby joey! Mama kangaroo's tail will help keep her standing upright, so take your time when assembling her so she (and her little Joey) can balance.

**Skill Level:** Easy ◼◼◻◻   **Finished Size:** Adult: approx 7" tall and 5" long   Joey: approx 2" tall and 1" long

## MATERIALS

Worsted-weight yarn in rusty brown (approx 150 yds), off-white (approx 50 yds), and black (approx 10 yds) **(4)**
Size G-6 (4 mm) crochet hook
8 mm or 9 mm black plastic eyes with safety backings for adult
6 mm or 7 mm black plastic eyes with safety backings for joey
4" x 6" piece of tan craft felt
Tapestry needle
Sewing needle and thread to match felt
Stuffing
Stitch markers to indicate beginning of rnds (optional)

## Adult Kangaroo

### HEAD

Starting with off-white yarn, make an 8-st adjustable ring (page 12).

Rnd 1: Sc 2 in each sc around. (16 sts)

Rnd 2: *Sc 3, sc 2 in next sc; rep from * 3 more times. (20 sts)

Rnd 3: Sc 20.

Change to brown yarn.

Rnds 4 and 5: Sc 20.

Rnd 6: *Sc 3, sc2tog; rep from * 3 more times. (16 sts)

Rnd 7: Sc2tog 8 times. (8 sts)

Rnd 8: In fl, sc 2 in each sc around. (16 sts)

Rnd 9: Sc 16.

Rnd 10: *Sc 7, sc 2 in next sc; rep from * 1 more time. (18 sts)

Rnd 11: Sc 18.

Rnd 12: Sc 1, *sc 3, sc 2 in next sc; rep from * 3 more times, sc 1. (22 sts)

Rnd 13: Sc 22.

Rnd 14: *Sc 10, sc 2 in next sc; rep from * 1 more time. (24 sts)

Rnd 15: Sc2tog 12 times. (12 sts)

Rnd 16: Sc2tog 6 times. (6 sts)

Stuff head and fasten off, leaving a long tail. Close up hole unless using plastic eyes.

### EAR (MAKE 2.)

Using brown yarn, ch 6.

Starting in 2nd ch from hook and working in back ridge loops, sc 2, hdc 2, dc 2 in back ridge loop of next ch. Rotate work. Starting in next ch and working in front loops, hdc 2, sc 2, sl st into next st and fasten off, leaving a long tail.

### BODY

Using brown yarn, make an 8-st adjustable ring.

Rnd 1: Sc 2 in each sc around. (16 sts)

Rnd 2: *Sc 3, sc 2 in next sc; rep from * 3 more times. (20 sts)

Rnd 3: *Sc 1, sc 2 in next sc; rep from * 9 more times. (30 sts)

Rnds 4–8: Sc 30.

Rnd 9: *Sc 1, sc2tog; rep from * 9 more times. (20 sts)

Rnd 10: Sc 20.

Rnd 11: *Sc 3, sc2tog; rep from * 3 more times. (16 sts)

Rnd 12: Sc 16.

Rnd 13: *Sc 2, sc2tog; rep from * 3 more times. (12 sts)

Rnd 14: Sc 12.

Rnd 15: *Sc 4, sc2tog; rep from * 1 more time. (10 sts)

Rnd 16: *Sc 3, sc2tog; rep from * 1 more time. (8 sts)

Stuff body.

Rnds 17–23: Sc 8.

Add more stuffing to tail.

Rnd 24: *Sc2tog, sc 2; rep from * 1 more time. (6 sts)

Rnds 25–27: Sc 6.

Add more stuffing to tail.

Rnd 28: Sc2tog 3 times. (3 sts)

Fasten off and weave in end.

### BACK LEG (MAKE 2.)

Starting with brown yarn, make a 6-st adjustable ring.

Rnd 1: Sc 3, sc 2 in next sc, sc 3 in next sc, sc 2 in next sc. (10 sts)

Rnd 2: Sc 3, *sc 2 in next sc; rep from * 6 more times. (17 sts)

Rnds 3–5: Sc 17.

Rnd 6: Sc2tog, *sc 1, sc2tog; rep from * 4 more times. (11 sts)

**Rnd 7:** Sc 1, *sc 3, sc2tog; rep from * 1 more time. (9 sts)

Change to off-white yarn.

**Rnds 8–12:** Sc 9.

Stuff and leave leg open. Fasten off, leaving a long tail.

### BACK FOOT (MAKE 2.)

Using off-white yarn, make a 6-st adjustable ring.

**Rnd 1:** Sc 3, sc 2 in next sc, sc 3 in next sc, sc 2 in next sc. (10 sts)

**Rnd 2:** Sc 3, *sc 2 in next sc; rep from * 6 more times. (17 sts)

**Rnd 3:** Sc 17.

**Rnds 4 and 5:** Sc in each sc around. (17 sts)

**Rnd 6:** Sc2tog, *sc 1, sc2tog; rep from * 4 more times. (11 sts)

**Rnd 7:** Sc 1, *sc 3, sc2tog; rep from * 1 more time. (9 sts)

**Rnds 8 and 9:** Sc 9.

Stuff feet.

**Rnd 10:** Sc 1, sc2tog 4 times. (5 sts)

Fasten off, leaving a long tail.

### ARM (MAKE 2.)

Starting with brown yarn, make a 4-st adjustable ring.

**Rnd 1:** In bl, sc in each sc around. (4 sts)

**Rnd 2:** *Sc 1, sc 2 in next sc; rep from * 1 more time. (6 sts)

**Rnds 3 and 4:** Sc 6.

Change to off-white yarn.

**Rnds 5 and 6:** Sc 6.

**Rnd 7:** In fl, sc 2 in each sc around. (12 sts)

**Rnds 8 and 9:** Sc 12.

**Rnd 10:** Sc2tog 6 times. (6 sts)

Stuff arm.

**Rnd 11:** Sc2tog 3 times. (3 sts)

Stuff and fasten off, leaving a long tail.

### FRONT POUCH

Using off-white yarn, make an 8-st adjustable ring.

**Rnd 1:** Sc 2 in each sc around. (16 sts)

**Rnd 2:** *Sc 3, sc 2 in next sc; rep from * 3 more times. (20 sts)

**Rnd 3:** Sc 6, sc 5 in next sc, sc 5, sc 5 in next sc, sc 7. (28 sts)

**Rnd 4:** Sc 8, *sc 2 in next sc; rep from * 2 more times, sc 7, **sc 2 in next sc; rep from ** 2 more times, sc 7. (34 sts)

Fasten off, leaving a long tail.

### ASSEMBLY

❶ Attach plastic eyes to sides of head, about 10 or 11 rnds from tip of nose, with 4 or 5 sts between them. Close hole at back of head. If you prefer, use black yarn to make French knots (page 16), or sew on felt circles for eyes. With black yarn, start under chin and shape cheeks by pulling yarn up through muzzle through top of rnd where color changes from off-white to brown. Loop yarn back under chin to start point and up through color change rnd again, pulling tightly to form 2 cheeks. Rep 3 or 4 times, ending at chin.

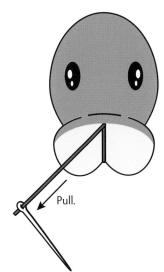

❷ With black yarn, embroider eyebrows above eyes using lazy daisy st (page 16), and nose using satin st (page 16). Embroider 3 satin sts on each side of cheek for whiskers over rnd where color changes from off-white to reddish brown. Attach ears above eyes and eyebrows. Cut 3 pieces of brown yarn, 3" long, and attach to top of head using fringe technique (page 19).

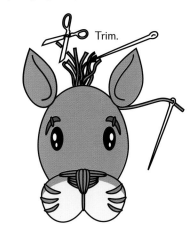

❸ With black yarn, form paws by drawing yarn through top of paw and then looping around to bottom 2 or 3 times, pulling tightly to cinch in front of paw. Rep 2 more times in different locations to form 4 fingers on paw. With black yarn, form toes by pulling yarn through front portion of foot around to bottom 2 or 3 times, pulling tightly to cinch in front of toe. Rep 2 more times in different locations to form 4 toes on foot. Attach open end of leg to top of foot at the ankle.

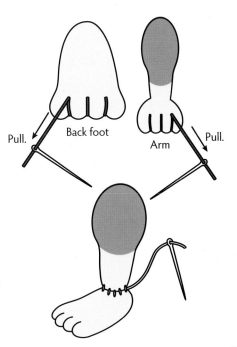

pouch and add a few more sts along pouch edge to hold rolled edge in place.

## Baby Joey

### BODY AND HEAD

Using brown yarn, make a 6-st adjustable ring.

Rnd 1: Sc 2 in each sc around. (12 sts)

Rnds 2 and 3: Sc 12.

Rnd 4: Sc2tog 6 times. (6 sts)

Rnd 5: Sc 2 in each sc around. (12 sts)

Rnd 6: Sc 12.

Rnd 7: *Sc 3, sc 2 in next sc; rep from * 2 more times. (15 sts)

Rnd 8: Sc 15.

Rnd 9: *Sc 3, sc2tog; rep from * 2 more times. (12 sts)

Rnd 10: Sc2tog 6 times. (6 sts)

Stuff and fasten off, leaving a long tail. Close up hole unless using plastic eyes.

### MUZZLE

Using off-white yarn, make a 4-st adjustable ring.

Sc 2 in each sc around. (8 sts)

Fasten off, leaving a long tail.

### EAR (MAKE 2.)

Using brown yarn, ch 6.

Starting in 2nd ch from hook, sc 1, hdc 2, dc 1, sl st in next ch.

Fasten off, leaving a long tail.

### LIMBS AND TAIL (MAKE 5.)

Using brown yarn, make a 4-st adjustable ring.

Sl st into next sc and fasten off, leaving a long tail.

### ASSEMBLY

❶ Attach ears to top of joey's head. Attach arm nubs to 4 corners of his body. Attach last nub to bottom of his back for a tail. Using belly-patch pattern (page 76), cut 1 patch from tan felt. Sew to joey's body. Stuff and attach muzzle to front of face.

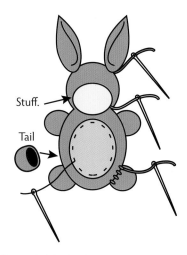

Stuff.

Tail

❷ With black thread, make a small lip cleft by making a vertical satin st from middle of bottom of muzzle, then up through to middle again, pulling gently. Embroider nose using satin st. Attach plastic eyes above muzzle. Close hole at top of head. If you prefer, use black yarn to make French knots, or sew on felt circles for eyes.

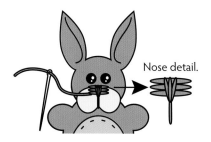

Nose detail.

❸ Pop the completed joey into his mother's pouch!

❹ Angle body sharply so tail can almost act like a third leg to help balance kangaroo when she stands. Attach head to top of neck. Attach legs about halfway up on body. To keep legs from splaying out, attach yarn to inside surface of one leg, pass yarn through body to inside surface of opposite leg, then back again through body to your starting point. Pull yarn gently to draw legs close to body before fastening off. Attach arms at shoulders of kangaroo.

❺ Using belly-patch pattern to fit (page 76), cut 1 patch from tan felt. With sewing needle and tan thread, sew belly using running st (page 16). Attach pouch to front of body using whipstitch (page 17) with flat edge of pouch open at the top. Fold over top lip of

# Zookeepers

No zoo can run without a crack team of zookeepers! These zookeepers are chock-full of great little details like jacket pockets, belts, rugged boots, and customizable hair. I recommend making them in DK-weight yarn if you've been sticking to worsted weight yarn for most of your zoo animals just to keep the size differences in a more accurate perspective.

**Skill Level:** Intermediate ◼◼◼◻     **Finished Size:** Approx 6" tall and 3" wide

## MATERIALS

DK-weight yarn ( 3 ) in:
  skin color (approx 50 yds),
  pant color (approx 25 yds),
  shirt color (approx 25 yds),
  hair color (approx 30 yds),
  yellow (approx 15 yds), and
  black (approx 15 yds)
Size E-4 (3.5 mm) crochet hook
6 mm or 7 mm black plastic eyes
  with safety backings
Small pieces of craft felt in brown,
  yellow, and color to match shirt
Tapestry needle
Sewing needle and thread to
  match felt
Embroidery thread for shoelaces
Stuffing
Stitch markers to indicate beginning of rnds (optional)

## Zoo Visitors

The zookeeper patterns could easily be used to create zoo visitors by changing yarn colors— and you could use sport-weight yarn and a size B-1 (2.25 mm) hook to make kids.

## HEAD

Using yarn for skin, make an 8-st adjustable ring (page 12).

**Rnd 1:** Sc 2 in each sc around. (16 sts)

**Rnd 2:** *Sc 3, sc 2 in next sc; rep from * 3 more times. (20 sts)

**Rnd 3:** *Sc 1, sc 2 in next sc; rep from * 9 more times. (30 sts)

**Rnd 4:** *Sc 4, sc 2 in next sc; rep from * 5 more times. (36 sts)

**Rnds 5–9:** Sc 36.

**Rnd 10:** *Sc 4, sc2tog; rep from * 5 more times. (30 sts)

**Rnd 11:** *Sc 1, sc2tog; rep from * 9 more times. (20 sts)

**Rnd 12:** *Sc 3, sc2tog; rep from * 3 more times. (16 sts)

**Rnd 13:** Sc2tog 8 times. (8 sts)
Stuff head.

**Rnd 14:** *Sc 2, sc2tog; rep from * 1 more time. (6 sts)

Fasten off, leaving a long tail for sewing. Close up hole unless using plastic eyes.

## NOSE

Using yarn for skin, make a 4-st adjustable ring.
Sl st into next sc and fasten off, leaving a long tail.

## EAR (MAKE 2.)

Using yarn for skin, make a 6-st adjustable ring. Ch 1 and turn.
Sk first ch, sc 6.
Sl st and fasten off, leaving a long tail.

## BODY

Starting with yarn for pants, make an 8-st adjustable ring.

**Rnd 1:** Sc 2 in each sc around. (16 sts)

**Rnd 2:** *Sc 3, sc 2 in next sc; rep from * 3 more times. (20 sts)

**Rnd 3:** *Sc 1, sc 2 in next sc; rep from * 9 more times. (30 sts)

**Rnds 4–6:** Sc 30.
Change to yarn for shirt.

**Rnds 7 and 8:** Sc 30.

**Rnd 9:** *Sc 1, sc2tog; rep from * 9 more times. (20 sts)

**Rnd 10:** Sc 20.

**Rnd 11:** Sc 1, with skin yarn sc 1, with shirt yarn sc 1, sc2tog, *sc 3, sc2tog; rep from * 2 more times. (16 sts)

**Rnd 12:** With skin yarn sc 3, with shirt yarn sc 13. (16 sts)
Change to yarn for skin.

**Rnd 13:** Sc2tog 8 times. (8 sts)
Stuff body.

**Rnd 14:** Sc2tog 4 times. (4 sts)
Fasten off, and weave in ends.

## BOOT TOP (MAKE 2.)

Using black yarn, make a 6-st adjustable ring.

**Rnd 1:** Sc 3, sc 2 in next sc, sc 3 in next sc, sc 2 in next sc. (10 sts)

**Rnd 2:** Sc 3, *sc 2 in next sc; rep from * 6 more times. (17 sts)

**Rnds 3–5:** Sc 17.

**Rnd 6:** Sc 1, sc2tog 8 times. (9 sts)

**Rnds 7 and 8:** Sc in each sc. (9 sts)

Stuff and fasten off, leaving a long tail.

## BOOT SOLE (MAKE 2.)

Using yellow yarn, make an 8-st adjustable ring.

**Rnd 1:** Sc 2 in each sc around. (16 sts)

**Rnd 2:** Sc 16.

**Rnd 3:** Hdc 2 in next sc, dc 2 in next sc, tr 2 in next sc, dc 2 in next sc, hdc 2 in next sc, sl st 9 and fasten off, leaving a long tail.

Attach to bottom of boot with RS facing out and hdc, dc, and tr sts oriented toward front of boot.

## THUMB (MAKE 2.)

Using yarn for skin, ch 6. Starting in 2nd ch from hook, sc 5.

Fasten off, leaving a long tail.

## HAND (MAKE 2.)

Using yarn for skin, make a 6-st adjustable ring. Ch 1 and turn.

Sk first ch, sc, hdc, dc, hdc, sc, sl st and fasten off, leaving a long tail.

## ARM (MAKE 2.)

Using yarn for skin, make a 6-st adjustable ring.

**Rnd 1:** Sc 3, hdc, dc, hdc. (6 sts)

**Rnd 2:** Sc 3, sc 2 in next sc, sc 3 in next sc, sc 2 in next sc. (10 sts)

Change to yarn for shirt.

**Rnd 3:** Sc in fl in each sc around. (10 sts)

**Rnd 4:** *Sc 3, sc2tog; rep from * 1 more time. (8 sts)

**Rnd 5:** Sc 8.

Stuff and fasten off, leaving a long tail.

Sew hand to end of arm with skin color, then sew thumb to inside of hand.

## ASSEMBLY

**❶** With the opening in the head facing down, attach plastic eyes 7 rnds from top of head with 5 sts between them. Close hole at bottom of head. If you prefer, use black yarn to make French knots (page 16), or sew on felt circles for eyes. Attach nose between eyes. Attach ears to sides of head in line with eyes and nose. Use yarn for hair to embroider eyebrows with lazy daisy st (page 16).

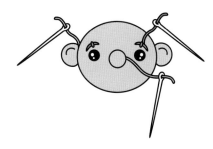

**❷** Attach head to body above neck. Flatten and sew open edges of arms shut with whipstitch. Sew arms to body. Sew on hand and thumbs to end of arms.

**❸** Add crochet details around cuffs and shirt (see "Crocheting on the Surface" on page 14). For cuffs, sc onto surface of arm directly over line separating shirt color from skin color. Cont all around until you reach first sc, sl st and fasten off. For shirt, use yarn for shirt color.

**Row 1:** Sc onto surface of body starting at front point of skin-colored triangle, and follow outline of skin color up and around neck. Cont sc down front of shirt until you reach 7 rnds from bottom (where pant color would be). Cont around circumference of body until you reach row of sc sts at front of body. Turn.

*Once you have reached the end of row 1, turn and begin row 2.

**Row 2:** Ch 2 (counts as first hdc), hdc in each sc around bottom of shirt until you reach front again, where sc turns upward toward collar. Cont sc in previous sts up to collar and around neckline, and back to starting position. Sl st in last sc and fasten off, leaving a long tail.

**❹** Using black yarn, pull yarn through body from back to front about 4 rnds from bottom of pants. Circle around bottom to back and repeat, pulling on yarn tightly to form 2 distinctive leg shapes. Pull yarn around and

through at least one more time
before fastening off.

Pull.

**5** Attach boots to bottom of legs.
Add shoelaces if desired, using
embroidery thread.

**6** Using patterns on page 77, cut
out 2 pockets from felt to match
shirt, 1 belt from brown felt, and
1 buckle from yellow felt. Fold top
of shirt pocket over and sew to
right and left sides of shirt using
a running st (page 16). Cut 2
small openings into buckles as
indicated on pattern and thread
belt through them. Trim belt to fit
around your zookeeper and sew it
in place.

Fold.

## Hair Options (from easy to challenging)

Using desired yarn for hair,
choose from the following techniques to finish your zookeeper.

### Bald

What could be easier? No yarn
required!

### Fringe hair

Using the "Fringe Technique"
on page 19, add as much or as
little hair as you like. To cover the
head of your zookeeper, 125 to
150 pieces of yarn, 3" to 4" long
should do the trick.

### Fun-fur fuzz

Using a novelty yarn like fun fur
is a great way to quickly get a
great fuzzy effect on the head of
your zookeeper. Attach yarn at the
back of the zookeeper's head and
single crochet onto the surface of
the head, covering the area where
you would like hair to be. Use a
slicker brush to help loosen hair

fibers before giving your zookeeper a haircut.

### Long hair

Loop the yarn around a small
5"–6" object, like a small picture
frame, 50 to 70 times. Cut one
side of the loop to make 10"- to
12"-long pieces of yarn. Divide the
yarn into groups of 8 to 10 pieces,
and use one strand to tie the
center of the group tightly, creating a bundle. Sew the bundles
onto the head, keeping the center
knots lined up to create a hair
part. Pull the hair into a ponytail,
leave it loose, or braid it.

## Tight curls

Attach hair-colored yarn to surface of head and sc 1. Repeat the following pattern: *slip stitch in surface st, ch 3, sk 2 sts, sc 1, rep from * until the head is filled with curls. Slip stitch and fasten off.

## Loop curls

Attach yarn to the surface and sc 1. *Loop working yarn over your index finger from front to back. Insert your hook through a surface stitch on the head and position the loop in front of the hook. Catch only the far side of the loop and pull through the surface stitch, taking care to avoid pulling the other side of the loop through as you go. There will now be two loops on your hook.

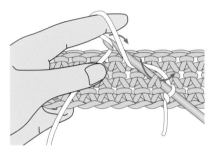

Bring the hook in front of the large loop and yarn over the hook with the working yarn. Pull the yarn through two loops on the hook. You'll have one loop on your hook and one large loop on the surface of your zookeeper's head.* Repeat from * to * to cover the head with loops.

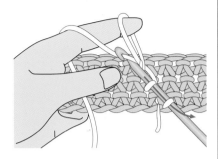

# Zoo Food

To make felt zoo food, use the patterns to cut shapes out of felt and turn them into steaks, fish, leaves, and bananas.

### FISH

From blue felt, cut out 2 fins, 1 fish front, and 1 fish back. Using sewing needle and blue thread, sew fish body together using whipstitch (page 17) or running st (page 16) and add a little stuffing before closing. Attach fins to each side using whipstitch. Using black thread, embroider an X on each side of fish's face for eyes.

### STEAKS

Cut out 2 steaks from red felt, 2 bones (rib-eye or T-bone) from white felt, and 1 edge strip from white felt. Turn 1 steak shape over so it mirrors the other and using a sewing needle and running st, attach bone shapes to front of steaks. Use whipstitch to sew steaks back to back and add a little stuffing before sewing them closed. Finally, fold edge strip halfway over edge of steak, and secure in place with running st around perimeter of steak, trimming to fit before finishing.

### BANANA

Cut out 1 banana from yellow felt. Match up edges and beg to sew sides tog using yellow thread and whipstitch. Add some stuffing before closing up, taking care to leave stem free. Once shape is stuffed and sewn together, use brown thread to embroider small star at bottom of banana and line of sts along each sewn edge.

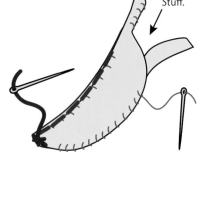

Stuff.

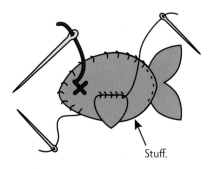

Stuff.

### LEAVES

Cut out 3, 4, or 5 leaves from green felt. Use dark-green thread to embroider leaf veins onto leaves. Arrange leaves in fan pattern and sew them tog into a group. If desired, make more leaves and sew several groups together.

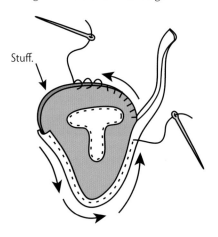

Stuff.

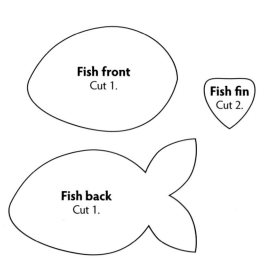

**Fish front**
Cut 1.

**Fish fin**
Cut 2.

**Fish back**
Cut 1.

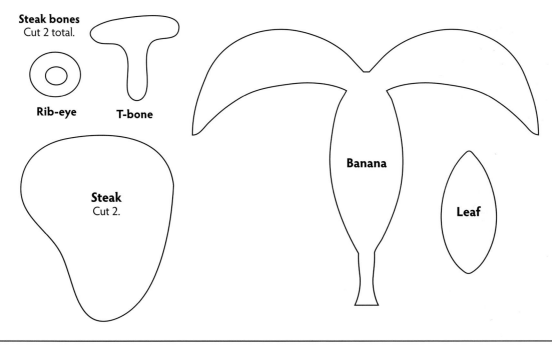

**Steak bones**
Cut 2 total.

**Rib-eye**     **T-bone**

**Steak**
Cut 2.

**Banana**

**Leaf**

**Steak edge** Cut 1.

*Trim end to fit.*

# Patterns

**Eyes**

5 mm   6 mm   7 mm   8 mm   9 mm   10 mm   11 mm   12 mm

**Multiple Pattern Sizes**
To help you get the perfect fit, some patterns are printed in multiple sizes so you can choose the most appropriately sized patch for your project.

**Patches**

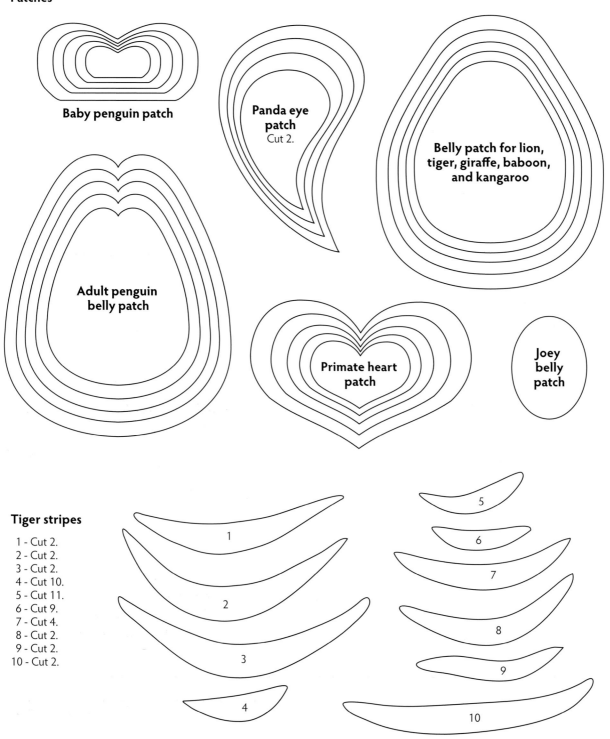

Baby penguin patch

Panda eye patch
Cut 2.

Belly patch for lion, tiger, giraffe, baboon, and kangaroo

Adult penguin belly patch

Primate heart patch

Joey belly patch

**Tiger stripes**

1 - Cut 2.
2 - Cut 2.
3 - Cut 2.
4 - Cut 10.
5 - Cut 11.
6 - Cut 9.
7 - Cut 4.
8 - Cut 2.
9 - Cut 2.
10 - Cut 2.

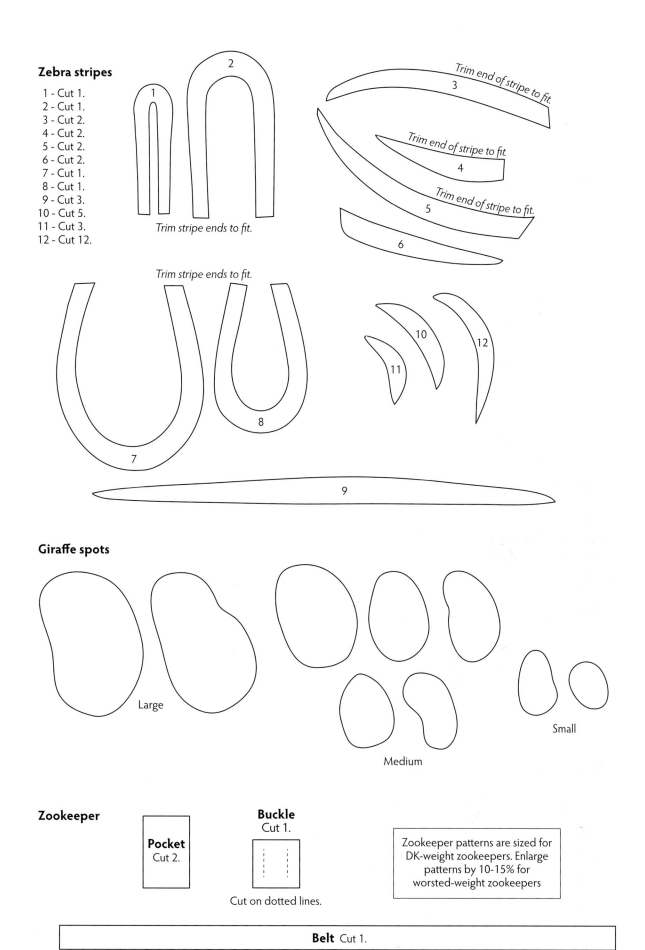

**Zebra stripes**

1 - Cut 1.
2 - Cut 1.
3 - Cut 2.
4 - Cut 2.
5 - Cut 2.
6 - Cut 2.
7 - Cut 1.
8 - Cut 1.
9 - Cut 3.
10 - Cut 5.
11 - Cut 3.
12 - Cut 12.

*Trim stripe ends to fit.*

*Trim end of stripe to fit.*

*Trim end of stripe to fit.*

*Trim end of stripe to fit.*

*Trim stripe ends to fit.*

**Giraffe spots**

Large

Medium

Small

**Zookeeper**

**Pocket**
Cut 2.

**Buckle**
Cut 1.

*Cut on dotted lines.*

Zookeeper patterns are sized for DK-weight zookeepers. Enlarge patterns by 10-15% for worsted-weight zookeepers

**Belt** Cut 1.

*Trim ends of belt to fit.*

# Useful Information

## ABBREVIATIONS

| | | | | | |
|---|---|---|---|---|---|
| * | Repeat instructions following the asterisk[s] as directed | dec(s) | decrease(ing)(s) | sc2tog | single crochet 2 stitches together—1 stitch decreased |
| approx | approximately | fl | front loop(s) | sk | skip |
| beg | begin(ning) | hdc | half double crochet(s) | sl | slip |
| bl | back loop(s) | inc(s) | increase(ing)(s) | sl st(s) | slip stitch(es) |
| CC | contrasting color | lp(s) | loop(s) | sp(s) | space(s) |
| ch(s) | chain(s) or chain stitch(es) | MC | main color | st(s) | stitch(es) |
| ch- | refers to chain, or chain space previously made, such as "ch-1 space" | mm | millimeter | tog | together |
| | | pm | place marker | tr | triple crochet |
| | | rep(s) | repeat(s) | WS | wrong side |
| cont | continue(ing)(s) | rnd(s) | round(s) | YO(s) | yarn over(s) |
| dc | double crochet(s) | RS | right side | yd(s) | yard(s) |
| | | sc | single crochet(s) | | |

## STANDARD YARN WEIGHTS

| Yarn-Weight Symbol and Category Name | **1** Super Fine | **2** Fine | **3** Light | **4** Medium | **5** Bulky | **6** Super Bulky |
|---|---|---|---|---|---|---|
| Types of Yarn in Category | Sock, Fingering, Baby | Sport, Baby | DK, Light Worsted | Worsted, Afghan, Aran | Chunky, Craft, Rug | Bulky, Roving |
| Crochet Gauge* Range in Single Crochet to 4" | 21 to 32 sts | 16 to 20 sts | 12 to 17 sts | 11 to 14 sts | 8 to 11 sts | 5 to 9 sts |
| Recommended Hook in Metric Size Range | 2.25 to 3.5 mm | 3.5 to 4.5 mm | 4.5 to 5.5 mm | 5.5 to 6.5 mm | 6.5 to 9 mm | 9 mm and larger |
| Recommended Hook in U.S. Size Range | B-1 to E-4 | E-4 to 7 | 7 to I-9 | I-9 to K-10½ | K-10½ to M-13 | M-13 and larger |

*These are guidelines only. The above reflect the most commonly used gauges and hook sizes for specific yarn categories.

## SKILL LEVELS

◼◻◻◻ **Beginner:** Projects for first-time crocheters using basic stitches; minimal shaping.

◼◼◻◻ **Easy:** Projects using yarn with basic stitches, repetitive stitch patterns, simple color changes, and simple shaping and finishing.

◼◼◼◻ **Intermediate:** Projects using a variety of techniques, such as basic lace patterns or color patterns; midlevel shaping and finishing.

◼◼◼◼ **Experienced:** Projects with intricate stitch patterns, techniques, and dimension, such as nonrepeating patterns, multicolor techniques, fine threads, small hooks, detailed shaping, and refined finishing.

## CROCHET HOOK SIZES

| Millimeter | U.S. Size* |
|---|---|
| 2.25 mm | B-1 |
| 2.75 mm | C-2 |
| 3.25 mm | D-3 |
| 3.5 mm | E-4 |
| 3.75 mm | F-5 |
| 4 mm | G-6 |
| 4.5 mm | 7 |
| 5 mm | H-8 |
| 5.5 mm | I-9 |
| 6 mm | J-10 |
| 6.5 mm | K-10½ |
| 8 mm | L-11 |
| 9 mm | M/N-13 |

*Letter or number may vary. Rely on the millimeter sizing.

# Resources

If you're interested in using some of the yarns or tools used in this book, please check out the following resources!

**Coats and Clark**
www.coatsandclark.com
Red Heart Yarns, available at local craft stores

**Lion Brand**
www.lionbrandyarn.com
Vanna's Choice Yarns, available at local craft stores

**Knit Picks**
www.knitpicks.com
Online retailer of fine yarns and notions

**Knitting, Beads, and Other Things**
www.knitbeads.com
US retailer of Sirdar Bonus DK

**Hobbs Bonded Fibers**
www.hobbsbondedfibers.com
Poly-down fiberfill toy stuffing and black batting, available at local craft stores

**NearSea Naturals**
www.nearseanaturals.com
Online retailer of sustainable, natural, and organic stuffing and thread

**6060**
www.6060.etsy.com
Online retailer of unique variety of plastic safety eyes

**Clover**
www.clover-usa.com
Hooks and notions, available at local craft stores

**Fiskars**
www.fiskars.com
Scissors and cutting mats, available at local craft stores

**American Felt and Craft**
www.americanfeltandcraft.com
Online retailer of fine wool felts and toy noisemaker inserts

## YARNS USED

The following yarns were used to make the toys in this book.

**Penguins**
Knit Picks Chroma worsted in Gray (25884) and Black (25884)
Knit Picks CotLin DK in Canary (24837)

**Harp Seal Adult**
Lion Brand Vanna's Choice in Linen (860-099) and Black (860-153)

**Harp Seal Baby**
Lion Brand Collection Angora Merino Yarn in Vanilla (491-098)
Knit Picks Brava Sport in Black (25663)

**Walrus**
Lion Brand Vanna's Choice in Honey (860-130), Black (860-153), and Beige (860-123)

**Polar Bear**
Red Heart Soft Yarn in Off-White (4601) and Black (4614)

**Grizzly Bear**
Red Heart Soft Yarn in Chocolate (9344), Wheat (9388), and Black (4614)

**Panda Bear**
Red Heart Soft Yarn in Off-White (4601) and Black (4614)

**Lion**
Red Heart Soft Yarn in Off-White (4601) and Wheat (9388)
Knit Picks Swish Worsted in Copper (23882)

**Lion Cub**
Sirdar Bonus DK in Oatmeal (964)
Knit Picks Brava Sport in Cream (25665) and Black (25663)
Knit Picks Swish Worsted in Copper (23882)

**Tiger**
Lion Brand Vanna's Choice in Rust (860-135) and Black (860-153)
Red Heart Soft Yarn in Off-White (4601)

**Rhinoceros**
Knit Picks Comfy Worsted Yarn in Seraphim (25317), Ivory (24162), and Black (25316)

**Elephants**
Knit Picks Brava Sport in Dove Heather (25666), Cream (25665), and Black (25663)
Knit Picks Brava Worsted in Dove Heather (25696), Cream (25695), and Black (25693)
Knit Picks Brava Bulky in Dove Heather (25726), Cream (25725), and Black (25723)

**Hippopotamus**
Knit Picks Comfy Worsted Yarn in Vinca (25320), Ivory (24162), and Black (25316)

**Zebra**
Red Heart Soft Yarn in Off-White (4601) and Black (4614)

**Giraffe**
Red Heart Worsted Weight Soft Yarn in Honey (9114), Chocolate (9344), Black (4614), and Off-White (4601)

**Gorilla**
Lion Brand Vanna's Choice in Silver Gray (860-149) and Black (860-153)

**Baboon**
Lion Brand Vanna's Choice in Taupe (860-125), Dusty Blue (860-108), Silver Blue (860-105), Colonial Blue (860-109), Cranberry (860-180), and Toffee (860-124)

**Chimpanzee**
Knit Picks Brava Sport in Black (25663)
Sidar Bonus DK in Flesh Tone (F013)

**Kangaroos**
Red Heart Soft Yarn in Off-White (4601) and Toast (E728)

**Zookeepers**
**Skin Colors:** Knit Picks Swish DK in Bark (24633) and Doe (24955)
Sirdar Bonus DK in Flesh Tone (F013)

**Hair Colors:** Knit Picks Swish DK in Cornmeal (24952), Coal (24045), Turmeric (25586), and Merlot Heather (no longer available in DK)
Knit Picks Swish Worsted in All Spice (24297)
Lion Brand Fun Fur Yarn in Chocolate (320-126)

**Clothing:** Knit Picks Brava Sport in Camel Heather (25668)
Knit Picks Swish DK in Dusk (24053), Moss (24057), and Squirrel Heather (24948)
Knit Picks CotLin DK in Coffee (24138)

**Shoes:** Knit Picks Swish DK in Coal (24045) and Cornmeal (24952)

# About the Author

mk crochet

Megan Kreiner grew up on Long Island, New York, in a household where art and art projects were a daily part of life. Coming from a long line of knitters and crocheters, Megan learned the craft at an early age from her grandmother, her aunt, and her mother, but only recently started to explore the wild and uncharted waters of pattern making.

A graduate with a fine arts degree in computer graphics and animation from the University of Massachusetts, Amherst, Megan is pursuing a career in the feature animation industry in Los Angeles. She is an artist and animator at DreamWorks Animation SKG. View her work at MKCrochet.com.

Megan lives in Altadena, California, with her husband, Michael, and son, James.

## Acknowledgments

First and foremost, thank you to my ever-patient husband for putting up with numerous skeins of yarn festooned around our home during the making of this book and for encouraging me in all aspects of my professional and personal projects. Thank you to my mother, Nancy; my grandmother Amelia, and my Aunt Marianne for teaching me to knit, crochet, and sew; and to both of my parents for nurturing my love of art as far back as I can remember. Thank you to my sister-in-law Amanda for suggesting I skip the premade patterns, throw caution to the wind, and design something on my own.

A big thank you to the publishing team at Martingale who took a chance on me and provided me with the opportunity to put this book together.

And, finally, thank you to my son, James, who inspires me to be creative every day.